BRITISH CASTLES

Alan Sorrell

B. T. BATSFORD LTD
London

To Elizabeth with love

First published 1973

Filmset by Keyspools Ltd, Golborne, Lancs
Printed in Great Britain by
William Clowes & Sons, Limited
London, Beccles and Colchester
for the publishers B. T. Batsford Ltd
4 Fitzhardinge Street, London W.1

ISBN 0 7134 1119 8

Contents

Acknowledgments

The author is most grateful to the following for their invaluable help in the preparation of this book: Mr K. J. Barton, Mr Arthur Corney, Mr Eric Holden, Dr Arnold Taylor, Dr R. Allen Brown, Mr Stuart Rigold, Dr Brian Hope-Taylor, Mr A. D. Saunders, Mr L. A. Helliwell, Mr A. D. Macleod, Mr O. E. Craster and Mr S. H. Cruden.
The author and publishers wish to thank the following for permission to reproduce illustrations appearing in this book: Mr Frank Todman for Rayleigh Mount; the Museum and Art Gallery, Worthing, for Bramber Castle; and the Portsmouth City Museums for Southsea Castle. The reconstruction of Pevensey Castle is the property of the artist; all other reconstructions and most of the photographs are Crown Copyright and are reproduced by permission of the Department of the Environment.

Bibliography

R. Allen Brown, H. M. Colvin and A. J. Taylor, *The History of the King's Works*
Hugh Braun, *The English Castle*
Armin Tuulse, *Castles of the Western World*
Derek Renn, *Norman Castles in Britain*
Brian Hope-Taylor, *Recent Archaeological Excavations in Britain*: The Norman Motte at Abinger and its Wooden Castle
Steven Runciman, *History of the Crusades*
Sidney Toy, *A History of Fortification*
Department of the Environment Guide Books

Introduction

When an object of any kind, a ship, a weapon, a garment or a building, becomes outdated or useless through changed conditions of life, fashion or purpose, it is invariably neglected or thrown on the rubbish heap. The old ship rots on the shore, the old sword rusts in its scabbard, the garment is crushed into the box in the dusty attic—and the building is despoiled. Its leaden roof is ripped off, the timbers decay and the windows swing on their hinges. Insidious ivy forces the stone walls apart and they totter and fall. But later still the old ship becomes an object of interest and its decks and bulwarks are lovingly restored, the old sword is drawn from its scabbard and becomes a prized possession, the garment is taken out of its box, is shaken very gently and begins its life anew in a museum case, a box of glass. As for the building—the Castle—it enters into its third state: no longer potent or terrifying, strong and protective, and no longer contemptuously neglected, it now in its old age becomes—picturesque. The ivy is stripped away, the walls buttressed, sometimes it is even reroofed. The transformation from decrepitude into a soft and gracious old age is complete and the evidence of the centuries of neglect and spoliation only adds a pleasing glamour to its stained walls and shattered turrets.

It is indeed remarkable that the stern and barbarous structures which we call 'castles' should be regarded with anything but repugnance. Were they to be erected today, there would be mass protests against such shocking violation of town and country amenities, and yet we love these grim ruins, despite their quite remarkable likeness in form and silhouette to some of the worst extravagances of our industrial age. Although we now have this curious affection for castles, it is probable that Cromwell received more credit than abuse when he ruthlessly 'slighted' the captured Royalist strongholds in the Civil War, precisely because they were then formidable, and therefore to be feared and destroyed whenever possible, like some ancient dinosaurs, archaic but still dangerous.

But the subject of castles bristles with more paradoxes than ever they did with pikes and spears on towers and battlemented walls in their heyday. There is, for instance, the paradox of appearance, for in their days of usefulness and splendour they had a look of brightness and gaiety utterly at variance with their terrifying purpose. We are fortunate in the survival of the Duc de Berry's *Très Riches Heures* in which the three Limbourg brothers present to us sensitive pictures of the medieval castle in its prime, just before the cannon began seriously to challenge the old order. All is beauty—of a highly sophisticated nature—gleaming white walls and towers, red-tiled or pale leaden roofs tipped with golden finials, pennons flying. Of course, this is idealization, too delicately insistent to carry absolute conviction, especially when one remembers that at that time France was suffering the anguish of the Hundred Years War. But idealization does at any rate show intent, and it is clear that it was the aim of the castle-builder to create such fantastically bright and gay structures. Incidentally, one of these miniatures depicts the castle of Vincennes with a number of seemingly isolated towers rising above a thick wood, and the effect is extraordinarily like the tower blocks of a twentieth-century city, all white and shining and set against a sky of ineffable blue. Hard reality must have presented a rather different kind of picture: the stench from garde-robes and sewage, and stagnant water in the ditch half-filled with decaying refuse, the discomfort of the cold and draughty rooms, window-slits boarded up, the harsh clank of iron on stone. And beneath all this the windowless dungeons where men died in darkness.

We are apt to think of the medieval castle as bustling with life, with steel caps at every merlon and loophole, and blaring trumpets and colourful heraldic insignia splattered everywhere. In fact, the normal garrison strength was very small, and as castle design became increasingly scientific with projecting bastions covering lengths of curtain wall, and cunningly devised gateways where the attackers were corralled into ravine-like passages, it became minimal. We are told that Harlech, the Edwardian concentric fortress where the principle of the mutual defensibility of each part of the fortress was developed to perfection, was defended by 37 men for a long period, and only fell to Owen Glendower 'in return for a sum of money' which is a polite definition of 'treachery'. Today everything has changed, the castles, from being highly coloured, odoriferous slums, have become dark but not desolate ruins, set in neatly trimmed lawns with postcard stalls in the rehabilitated guard-rooms, and with an intermittently swarming population of plodding sightseers, who would outnumber by 20 to one any medieval garrison who might be brought back from the shades to witness this extraordinary reversal of all the values associated with castles as known to them.

A castle has been described as a 'fortified mansion', which sounds slightly pompous if applied to a motte-and-bailey castle, and totally inadequate if related to, say, the Tower of London. But as a formula it does help to narrow the subject to manageable proportions, and at one stroke of the dictionary maker's pen we can rule out the huge fortified camp or 'cantonment' type of fortification whose function was the safeguarding of groups of barrack buildings and administrative and storage complexes: very early examples have come to light in the Middle East—Assyria—and in the wastes of Nubia, and the Romans adopted the principle for their great legionary forts and lesser fortifications all over the empire. But in northern Europe and Britain it is an imposed pattern: it would seem that we do not like absolute regularity and diffusion but prefer concentration and some degree of asymmetry. The commandant's house in a legionary camp was in no sense 'a fortified mansion', but only one stone-built structure amongst others, the headquarters, the hospital, the tribunes' houses, the workshops, the stables and the barrack blocks. The same may be said of the Assyrian Fort Shalmanesar at Asshur and the Egyptian fortress at Buhen, where the same confusing regularity would have been found. It must have been very easy to lose one's way in those huge impersonal military beehives. And there, perhaps, is the crux of the matter and real justification for commencing this study of British castles with the Norman Conquest, for then, for the first time, the castle became something personal to whoever built and lived in it, and not just the expression of some far-off impersonal authority.

It does seem, indeed, that pompous or inadequate though it may be, 'fortified mansion' does express a salient truth, that a true castle must have its hard defensive core, its 'mansion', whether it be keep, great fortified gateway or motte. It is an interesting point to note that the Assyrian, Egyptian and Roman fortresses had hard outer skins and soft cores—or no cores at all. The defensive force was stationed on the strong curtain wall and bastions. This meant a most extravagant use of manpower, but it also indicated immense confidence, in that retreat to an inner line or citadel was outside the scope of ancient military thought. With the medieval castle, however, it would almost seem that the defenders expected to be driven back from one strong defensive line to another and that knight and man-at-arms, encased from head to foot in plate-armour or chain mail, were for ever looking over their shoulders towards that massive keep or strong point which, with or without justification, gave hope of impregnable security. We must not ignore the relative strength of the attack in ancient and medieval times, and the later defenders may well have been relatively weaker than the earlier warriors in spite of their huge fortifications, but the Roman plan (as has been suggested above) surely reflects faith in the invincible majesty of the old order, a faith which persisted long after the empire had slipped down into ruin. But the medieval robber baron, earl or king had none of this sublime self-confidence and one cannot escape the feeling that in the final analysis these castles were little more than bolt-holes—though often highly ornamental ones. We know that 'an Englishman's house is his castle' (or was until recently when the compulsory-purchase orders made his tenure less secure): he locks the front door and waits for the would-be intruder to go away, he avoids the windows and probably retires to an inner room. He is not a robber baron, and his house is not a bolt-hole, but the instinct for security, however fallacious, is age-old!

When the Roman legions withdrew from Britain in the early fifth century they left behind them, intact, so far as we know, a massive system of defence on every coast and along the northern frontier of the provinces, and not until Norman times was Britain so well provided with fortresses and military works of all kinds. Reasonably enough, the rapid success of the Norman invaders has been attributed to the almost complete absence of strong points where the Saxons, badly bruised at Senlac, could have regrouped their still potentially powerful forces. An argument valid for 1066 should, theoretically, explain the reason for the slow Saxon advance in the fifth and sixth centuries, but in fact the two conquests were totally different in character: the Norman was a single powerful thrust under one leader, whilst the Saxon was more in the nature of gradual piecemeal infiltration, sometimes as allies of the Britons, and often fighting amongst themselves, and it is unlikely that the Britons had the men or the united will to take advantage of their inherited fortifications. Only in the west, in the sixth century under the legendary Arthur, did the Britons rally for a time, and it is interesting to record that Cadbury Rings, an Iron Age hill fort captured by Vespasian in 43 A.D., has recently been the scene of excavation and is enthusiastically spoken of as the site of 'many-towered Camelot'. If this claim could be established it would certainly indicate that the Britons, far from defending their stone-walled fortresses, had indeed taken to the hills. We have all seen photographs of deserted military buildings at Aden and elsewhere, squatters in possession, and a pervading air of shabby progressive decay, and this is probably what happened to the Roman military works in Britain.

Signal-stations (or watch-towers) were built by the Romans in Britain not only in the late third century to combat the increasing menace of raiding Saxon galleys, but at an early date (50 A.D.) in Devonshire, and about 70 A.D. by Agricola, who erected a closely connected series in Perthshire. It is these early examples which are of peculiar interest to us because of their extraordinary likeness in design and form to the constructions we know as 'motte-and-bailey castles' which came to Britain 1,000 years later with the conquering Normans. Four or six posts arranged in a rectangular plan with a circular surrounding ditch and stockade is the usual layout both for the early Roman signal-stations and the primitive Norman motte-and-bailey castle. Later Roman

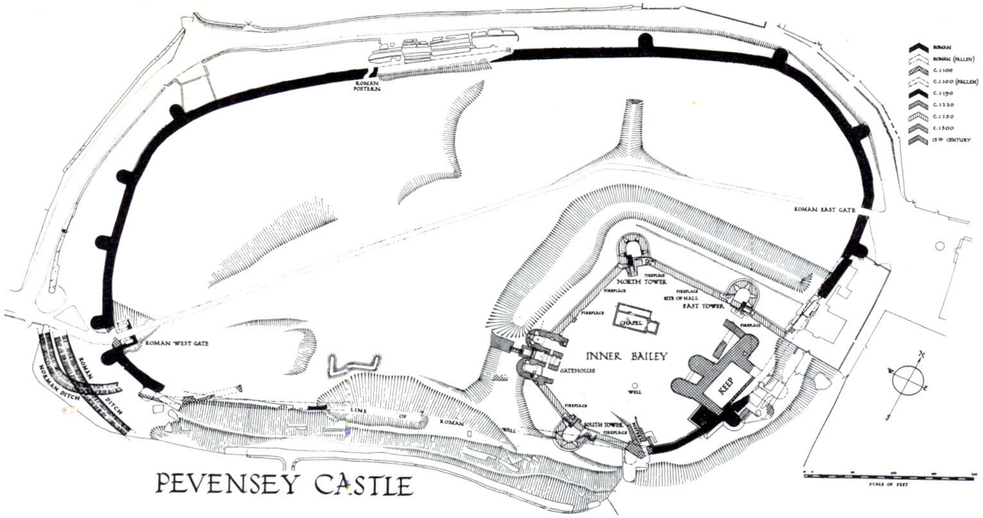

PEVENSEY CASTLE

examples are much more elaborate and massively stone-built. A relief on Trajan's Column (*c.* 100 A.D.) shows a Dacian timber watch-tower closely resembling the Roman signal-stations, and it is possible that the Romans at an earlier date had adopted this east European type which they subsequently used as a standard defence unit. Later, when the frontier defences were overwhelmed (it is on record that there were at least 1,000 of these towers on the German frontier alone), the idea of the stilted tower must have been introduced into Gaul by Gothic and Frankish invaders. There is no evidence for the motte in the Roman examples known to us, excepting that the ground level within the enclosing ditch was automatically raised by the excavated earth being thrown inwards, but by the time of the Bayeux Tapestry it had become common practice, as the embroidered pictures of Dinan, Dol and Hastings clearly show. It is an ironic thought that under the English turf, destroyed by their barbarian ancestors, lay the ruins of these miniature castles, whose resurrection in a slightly developed form was a potent weapon in the enslavement of the Anglo-Saxon people by their Norman foe. One's sympathies are always with the defeated, but when one considers the singular obtuseness of the Saxon military mind, sympathy gives place to an irritable feeling of astonishment. The dash south of the exhausted army after its victory at Stamford, the bungling inactivity of the fleet, the refusal to pursue a 'scorched earth' policy, and finally the decision to stake all on a battle, all these were mistakes of the campaign, and probably of Harold himself, but the Saxon attitude towards fortification was deep-seated and fatal. The stockade surrounding the burgh seems to have been the limit of their imagination, and vanity and a kind of valorous stupidity compelled them to rely on the shield-wall as a sufficient defence against all who might come against them.

Pevensey Castle

Pevensey, the Anderida of the Romans, was captured by the Saxons in 491, when, according to the Anglo-Saxon Chronicle, there was a great slaughter of the Britons. This is the only recorded instance of a Saxon assault on a fortified place, and it must have been an occurrence of an altogether exceptional nature in the long-drawn-out invasion of Britain.

In Roman times Pevensey was one of the series of fortresses built in the second half of the third century to defend the eastern and southern coasts of Britain: we know them as Saxon Shore Forts. Pevensey, or Anderida as it should be called in this connection, was egg-shape in plan, and quite untypical of Roman fortification where the rectangle was the usual and the trapezoid the occasional pattern. The site was well-chosen, approachable by land only from the south west, and guarded at that point by two solid bastions projecting beyond the single gate with its two rectangular guard-rooms set back behind the wall, along which round-fronted bastions were set at irregular intervals, so that all the intervening wall faces could be covered by the fire of the defenders. Ten of these solid bastions still survive. There was an east gate which led on to a causeway giving access to the harbour where a squadron of galleys or scouting craft was stationed. No doubt Anderida was connected with the other Saxon Shore Forts at Lympne, Dover, Richborough and Reculver on the east and Portchester on the west by a series of signal-stations, although in fact no trace of them has been discovered. The sea has long since receded from Pevensey—though it is now creeping in again—but up to the early Middle Ages it could still be reckoned as a port, and the fortress would never have been built or maintained for so long but for its harbour. Originally the interior of the fort was filled with rows of barrack-blocks and administrative buildings, all presumably of timber construction since no trace of stone foundations have survived. It is an interesting fact that whilst earlier works such as the forts on Hadrian's Wall and the great legionary fortresses at Caerleon and Chester show important indications of stone-built barrack-blocks, no such remains have been found in any of the later Saxon Shore Forts, where the major effort was concentrated on the defences. Perhaps this substitution of wood for stone was a sign of the declining prosperity of the imperial finances, but even so, the achievement was an extravagant one: walls 25 feet high and 12 feet thick, the rubble core faced with courses of green sandstone and iron-stone, enclosed an area of about eight acres, a formidable soft-core fortress. Thereafter is no mention of the still strong fortress until 1066. Then William, landing nearby, stumbling on the shingle, and grasping the land of England with both his hands, filled Pevensey Castle with his men.

Within the circuit of the Roman walls there may well have been Saxon dwellings, and the foundations of a pre-conquest chapel survive in the Inner Bailey of the medieval castle. It was in this south-east corner of the old fortress that William assuredly established his strongpoint and defended it with a ditch and stockade. Nothing could have been more typical of the dullness of the Saxon military mind than the neglect of this ready made fortress with its important harbour—the ideal base for an invader. Later Pevensey was granted by William to his half brother Robert, Count of Mortain, who constructed a castle which was, one supposes, a development of William's earlier strongpoint. Then, *c.* 1130 a remarkable stone keep replaced the timber structure, and it had no less than five round-fronted bastions, and also incorporated, for good measure, a Roman bastion at its south-east angle. Obviously the strength and efficiency of these Roman bastions had impressed the medieval builders to the point of obsession, and this becomes even more marked when we find that the stone curtain wall surrounding the inner bailey, added about a century later, was also strengthened with round-fronted gatehouse towers and bastions which are twice the size of their ancient predecessors. But the particular interest of Pevensey (as with Portchester) is that it tides over the long night of Saxon England—that is, so far as fortification is concerned—and links Roman forts with Norman motte-and-bailey and the great medieval castles in the chain of a common tradition.

The motte-and-bailey castle was the visible symbol of conquest; the Saxons must have seen with astonishment and despair these raw earthen mounds topped with stockades and wooden towers whitewashed or garishly coloured, and sometimes the flash of arms which told of an unsleeping, alert and oppressive power. There can be no doubt that Saxon slave labour painfully created these mottes and so they had the mortification of being the engineers of their own harsh fate. Within a very few years of the conquest the whole land, town, village and countryside, was dominated by these strange alien forms, although for the men of Wessex the circular motte-mounds must have brought to their minds the funerary monuments, the tumuli, of prehistoric man. Maybe Silbury Hill, towering and solitary, became almost an emblem of their own defeat. Nothing like this spate of building and digging had happened in Britain since the Romans came almost exactly 1,000 years before.

The castles of the conquest, alien although they may have been, were an expression, however harsh and unwelcome, of disciplined power and order, and there was an undoubted rationality in their numbers and siting, but very different was the state of affairs in 1150, for by then the symbol of power had proliferated into a swarming curse. Castles were built everywhere by a baronage which had broken every bond, delighting in civil war and defying the weak King Stephen, and if we are to believe the Anglo-Saxon Chronicle (which finally came to an end at this time), 'Every castle was filled with devils and evil men'. The anarchy was abruptly terminated by the masterful young King Henry on his accession in 1154 when he ordered the wholesale destruction of these unlicensed or 'adulterine' castles.

What little we know of the appearance of the early motte-and-bailey castle derives from the Bayeux Tapestry, that matchless contemporary pictorial record, some contemporary written accounts (though the best of these refer to continental castles), sculpture and, lastly, excavation. From the latter source, we now know that in its most primitive form the castle's great vertical supporting stilts were first erected with their lower ends resting on stone rubble, or some such stable material, and the earth was then heaped around them to form the motte. The ditch from which the earth was dug automatically increased its height. In confirmation of this recently deduced theory, the Bayeux Tapestry shews workmen heaping up earth around and under the newly assembled prefabricated Hastings Castle. It is obvious, of course, that many of the mottes were based on natural hillocks or rock formations so that the vertical timbers, encased in only a few feet of heaped and battened earth may be said to have been founded on the natural 'datum line'—although the castle might be raised perhaps 70 feet above the surrounding plain. At Totnes there is a very large motte, partly natural rock but the bulk of it artificial. On the summit stood a tower, square in plan. 'This stood on a dry-stone foundation, which has been traced down for 11 feet into the body of the motte' . . . 'This foundation was evidently built up with the motte to provide a firm foundation for the tower' (Rigold) which was probably of timber. Dr Hope-Taylor in his report on his excavation of the Abinger motte refers to slotted horizontal timbers which lay at or below the surface to give stability to the structure, and devices of various kinds were employed, no doubt, to achieve this end. The tower of the latter was almost absurdly small, only 12 feet square, but probably judging from the size of its post holes, relatively lofty. No 'mansion' this, but the precursor of the more splendid towers which were to come. This Abinger tower was surrounded by a stockade provided with a wall walk, and pierced by a single entrance not in alignment with the ladder or gangway up the side of the motte. This ladder was reached by a bridge spanning the ditch, in its turn surrounded by a stockade, and beyond this, stockaded embankments and ditches enclosing the bailey where stood the domestic buildings, stables and storehouses which made up the castle complex.

Pevensey Castle, as it might have appeared in 1066

In thinking of the smaller motte-and-bailey castles, one is conscious of a curiously unrealistic quality, or perhaps one might describe it as a feeling of desperation, in the extremely limited size of these little isolated wooden-boxes perched on their earthen mounds. Direct assault up the steep slopes would have been daunting to the attackers weighed down with armour and weapons, under a hail of missiles, but starvation has always been a potent instrument of war, and these towers could have been little less than traps unless outside help was certain and speedy. But that they were intended as final points of resistance is indeed suggested by the rectangular markings, each one with a round boss in its centre, which are shown in a carved capital originally in Westminster Hall and now in the Victoria and Albert Museum. These markings cover the whole surface of the tower, and Hope-Taylor thinks that the round bosses with their central holes may have been, in effect, loopholes through which the defenders could have thrust spears at their attackers. There are five rows of these rectangular shapes and it is difficult to estimate scale. Does each row represent a floor? It is most unlikely—five floors in a wooden building is not even a possibility. Perhaps one can visualise two spear holes to each floor, at knee and shoulder height, with the fifth under the battlements. In the Bayeux Tapestry where the attacks on the motte castles at Dol and Dinan are shewn, a chequer board effect is achieved with the rectangular shapes. Disappointingly, no thrusting spears occur in either of these attacks: mounted men charge up to the flimsy flying bridge at Dol, a charming fantasy this—one cannot expect the Saxon ladies who embroidered the tapestry to be always right in their facts of war—and foot soldiers apply burning brands, whilst the defenders hurl their spears from conspicuously exposed positions on the castle top. No siege engines are shown, presumably scaling ladders and battering rams were the only devices needed before the construction of stone castles, though even these are not to be found in the Tapestry.

We often see, in the no doubt well authenticated films of the American west of less than 100 years ago stockaded forts (but without the mottes) very similar in type to their Norman predecessors of 900 years earlier, and it is to be hoped that a careful study and record has been made and kept of these modern fortifications which in purpose and type so closely follow an ancient tradition. But it is a mistake to associate motte-and-bailey castles, or castles of any age solely with the idea of war and siege and assault. The early castles originally planted to overawe the defeated Saxons soon became the homesteads or mansions of the local magnates. Probably garrisons still 'stood to' but it is not difficult to imagine the gradual change of function which must have taken place—although there was a dreadful reversal of this peaceful process in the anarchy of Stephen's reign, but in spite of this and other set-backs the process went on. An important, even vital point which should be made, is that unlike the Roman (or the American) forts, the post-conquest castles of Britain were privately owned. Admittedly there were Royal castles too, but nationwide these were only a small minority, and significantly, they were built, in nearly every instance, to overawe the towns and cities, and so left the countryside where the bulk of the population lived, virtually in the hands of the magnates, great and small, good and bad. This meant, on the one hand, concentration of the central authority in the towns dominated by the Royal castles, and on the other hand, increased vitality, diversity of character and sturdy self-reliance elsewhere—and eventually to those Knights of the Shires who went to Westminster to speak up for their own people.

Rayleigh Mount

Rayleigh Castle, (page 11) which is known by the more descriptive name of 'Rayleigh Mount' is a typical and interesting motte-and-bailey castle, and has recently been the subject of a report of excavations carried out from 1959 onwards. It is recorded in Domesday Book, was extended by Henry of Essex *c.* 1180, and was further developed *c.* 1290. Thereafter it fell into decay. So this primitive and simple type of castle survived for some 300 years, into the reign of King Edward I, the builder of the greatest and most sophisticated British castles. There is no evidence that stone buildings or fortifications ever existed at Rayleigh, though the motte was revetted with ragstone and flint rubble, presumably to stabilise the loamy clay and prevent erosion by rain channelling its soft surface. Rayleigh Mount is a significant instance of the overlapping of building method and the survival of ancient forms—and within 35 miles of London. Excavation has disclosed an elaborate timber bridge and barbican for the defence of the entrance to the bailey. The bridge, rising from the outer lip of the great ditch, was 120 feet in length and no less than 16 feet in width, and supporting timbers from the lowest part of the ditch must have been 20 feet in height. The semicircular barbican stood on a flat topped artificial mound beyond the ditch, and nearly 20 feet below the level of the bailey. A drawbridge led to the outer gate and substantial stockades with wall-walks defended the passage through this gate to the bridgehead. Access to the bridge was by a second drawbridge at a steeply inclined plane and was at an angle difficult for a horseman to negotiate, and nearly impossible for a laden cart. The design of these stockaded defences is peculiar in that they all face the same way, as though the military engineers could envisage attack from only one direction, leaving the defenders' backs as excellent

Rayleigh Mount, as it might have appeared in the late thirteenth century

Alan Sorrell 1970

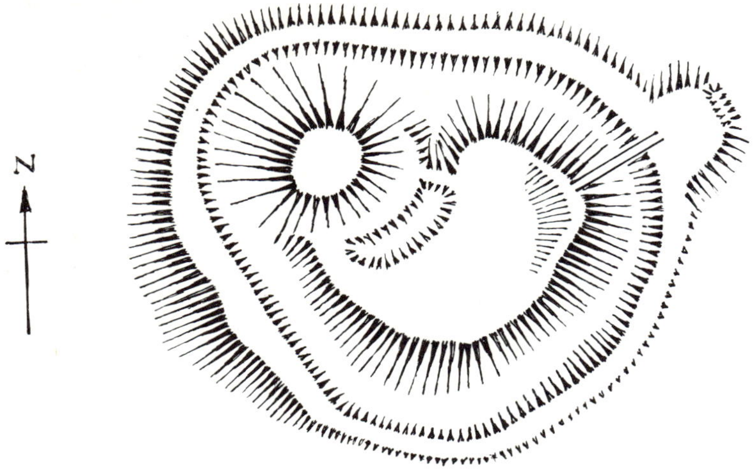

RAYLEIGH MOUNT c. 1172

targets for arrows of attackers with other ideas. (On a vastly different scale, and 900 years later, one is reminded of the defences of Singapore, with the batteries so arranged that the enemy, attempting a sea-borne assault, would be blown to smithereens. In the event the Japanese disobligingly attacked from the landward side and the fortress fell.) So far as we know, the defences of Rayleigh Castle were never put to test of war and the barbican rotted in peace: it should be added that the work was done under the threat of baronial revolt in 1173, at a total cost of £25 19*s* 5*d*, and this was borne by the Crown, for the castle had reverted to the King in 1163. Castle builders of all ages have devoted an inordinate amount of attention to gateway design, often neglecting the danger of flank attack and the consequent bypassing of all their concentration of effort. In Edwardian times, this obsession reached the ultimate by turning the gate defences into the central strongpoint of the fortress: Harlech is a good example of this extra-ordinary metamorphosis.

At Rayleigh, in common with the great majority of motte-and-bailey castles, the motte was placed so that it was on the edge of the fortified area, and this curious arrangement, where the strongpoint was located in an exposed and indeed vulnerable position has never been satisfactorily explained. It might have been expected that the principle of the concentric castle would have become obvious long before it did, but any form, once established is hard to break, and so it was in this case. It has been suggested that the motte with its tower was sited so as to command the bailey defences, and at the same time offer an escape route into the open country for a disheartened garrison. But who can really imagine a defeated crowd of men-at-arms, some wounded, all exhausted, with, perhaps, women and children, slithering down the steep motte side—into the unwelcoming arms of the besiegers waiting below—and all except the last contingency as part of an organised, and anticipated, manoeuvre? This curious arrangement of motte-and-bailey persisted into medieval times, and Flint, the first castle of Edward I's strategic Welsh castle building programme, carries on the tradition, as does the French Coucy, which is generally regarded as its pattern (of a slightly earlier date). Perhaps the northern passion for asymmetry, a certain unclassical casualness, may be responsible for the oddity.

No long time elapsed between motte-and-wooden-towers, and their translation into motte-and-stone-walls, or what are known as shell-keeps. As it is unlikely that stone walls would have been imposed upon newly-heaped earth, even though they were often, perhaps generally strengthened by platforms of oak beams, layers of rammed chalk or clay, gravel or flint rubble, it must be clear that the earlier versions of the shell-keep were built on natural hillocks or rock foundations. Shell-keeps form the nucleus of a high proportion of British castles, and in some cases they are so embellished and disguised that they are difficult to recognise: the Round Tower of Windsor Castle is an example of such a transformation. The original structure, a massive retaining wall, 12 feet thick, and still surviving to a height of 15 feet, was built by the Conqueror on a natural foundation which has been described as 'the only strong point in the Thames Valley between London and Wallingford where a fortress could be built'. This genuine, typical shell-keep, 130 feet in diameter, was constructed of the local sandstone, has a pronounced batter, and was strengthened by flat pilaster buttresses. Within this wall Henry II erected another, overtopping the Norman work by 34 feet, and it too was strengthened with wide buttresses. Inside this great ovoid shell-keep were timber buildings, probably of two storeys and there was a central square courtyard. Then in 1826 came the final addition of 30 feet in height. As it stands today the Round Tower is more a monument to the Gothic Revival and Sir John Wyattville (the 'ville' was added to give an appropriate medieval quality to the name) than to William the Conqueror and his medieval successors.

However, despite this nineteenth century extravaganza, the original form has survived, and one can say of Windsor that the shell-keep has been transformed rather than disguised.

Norman Windsor had two baileys, with the shell-keep standing between them, an unusual arrangement, though Arundel had a comparable plan. It is thought likely, however, that one of the baileys may be a later addition, and if that was so, Windsor takes its place with the majority of motte-and-bailey and shell-keep castles in the conventionality of its plan. A high proportion of shell-keeps are to be found in the southern half of England, and several examples are in the south-west—Totnes, Restormel, Tremarton, Launceston, Barnstaple—and they are especially interesting because they show such wide variations of a common type. We are apt to think of the Normans, as we do of their intellectual (though not their racial) ancestors, the Romans, as having a marked rigidity of approach to their military problems, but when we think of their earthen mottes and wooden towers, their shell-keeps, their enormous rectangular stone keeps and round towers, it becomes evident that they did have a surprising capacity for adapting themselves to all kinds of circumstances, topographical, tactical and political. An appreciation of these 'circumstances' leads one to study the implications of the siting of the various types of castle: why, for instance, should there be a great stone tower where a shell-keep would appear to have been equally effective? It has been said that there was more comfort and security in the great towers, but a strongly walled shell-keep on a rocky hill, such as Totnes, assuming the existence of the vital water supply, was at least as secure. Not until the development of the projectile throwers, trebuchets, mangonels and catapults towards the end of the twelfth century could the relatively open shell-keep be thought of as defensively inferior—though after this time the destructive plunging fire of these weapons must have put a premium on high, strongly roofed castles. But earlier, there can be no doubt that these rectangular keeps were not only very strong, but, to friend and foe alike, were extremely impressive symbols of dominating power, and valuable as such, and it may well be that they were erected where such emphasis was most needed.

There was an enormous concentration of motte-and-bailey castles along the Welsh border and in Pembroke—'Little England beyond Wales' as it has been called—and a high proportion of the remainder were in the Midlands, with relatively few in the east and south-east, whilst the majority of the shell-keeps are to be found in the south and west as noted above. Rectangular tower-keeps were heavily concentrated in the south-east—Colchester, Hedingham, London, Rochester, Canterbury, Dover, Pevensey; another group in the north, Carlisle, Newcastle, Bamburgh, Scarborough, Appleby, Brough, Bolsover, Bowes and Richmond; a smaller group on the Welsh border and along the line of the Severn; and the remainder sparsely sprinkled over the rest of the country. It would be satisfactory if one could theorise about this distribution and conclude that the south-eastern concentration, keyed into Dover, was to secure the route to the Continent, and at the same time safeguard London against invasion from Scandinavia. That the latter was a real peril is clear when one recollects the destruction of Colchester by the Danes in 1071, and that its keep was built to prevent a repetition of that disaster. The safeguarding of communications between England and Normandy was clearly of vital importance and something no Norman king dare neglect, and William the Conqueror fortified Dover immediately after the Battle of Hastings. Even before the Conquest it was defended by earthworks, probably in the Norman manner. The northern fortresses guarded the coast at Newcastle, Bamburgh and Scarborough on the east, and Carlisle on the west, with the string of smaller castles across the Pennines as a defence against the Scots, and the west country group defended the valley of the Severn and the Midlands against the Welsh. Was there then, a dominating military and political intelligence capable of laying down the broad lines of a defensive scheme which not only took into account invasion from beyond the frontiers, but also the necessity of dominating a restless subject population? William comes instantly to mind as the obvious candidate, a man who could scheme so rightly and with such compelling force that long after his death his successors went on developing a policy which had the inevitability of genius.

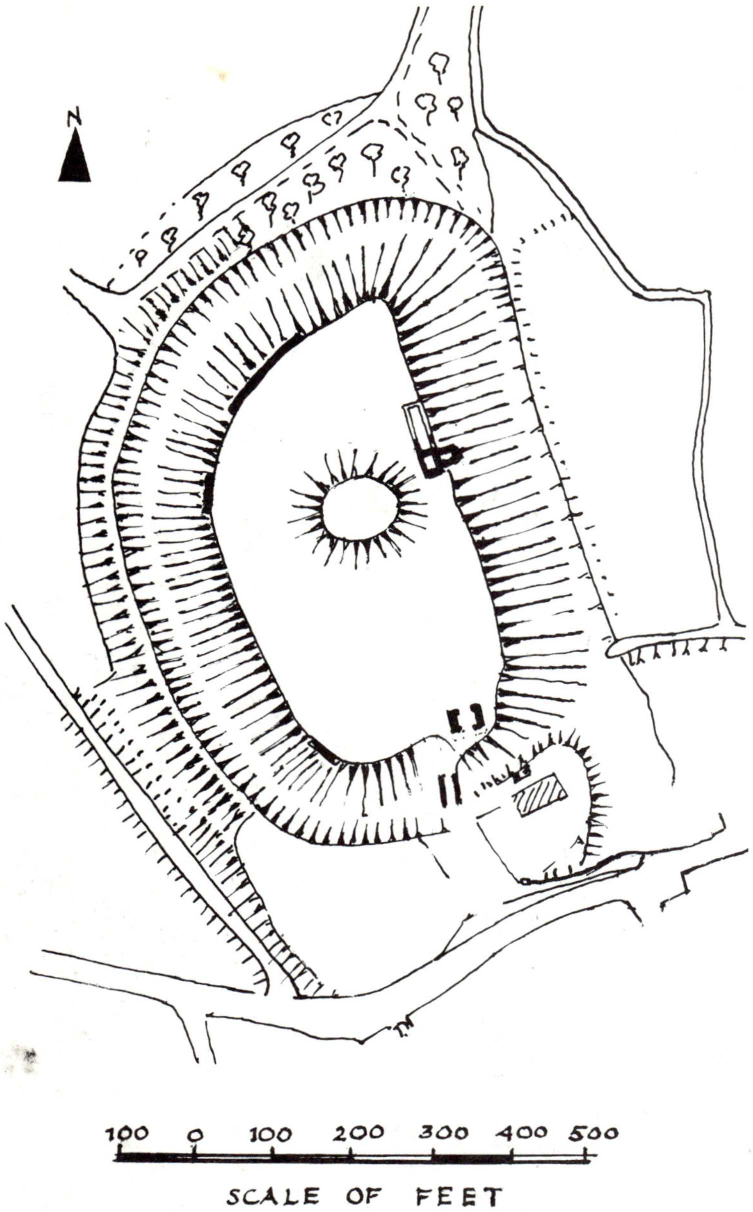

Bramber Castle

Bramber Castle, rising high above the wide, once marshy valley of the Adur in Sussex, is a transitional motte-and-bailey castle with some unusual features. The site is a natural stronghold, and with its slopes scarped it became unassailable, except from the south, but there it was cut off from the gentler slope by a deep ditch which continued, at an increased depth around the whole site. Originally the motte stood in a central position in the bailey, but this was modified when the east side was straightened *c.* 1100. The filled-in surrounding ditch is still visible as a slight depression. This motte, and the timber tower and palisade which, it is reasonable to suppose, surmounted it, were soon abandoned, and a gate-house, of flint and stone construction, and measuring approximately 38 by 40 feet, pierced by an entrance gateway took its place. A battlemented flint and stone outer curtain complete with wall-walk was built, and that the constructional skills of the Normans (or their Saxon serfs) were not always of a very high order is shewn by the indications of rebuilding due to faulty work. Gatehouse tower and curtain can be dated about 1100, then, in 1140 the entrance archway was blocked so that the structure could support the weight of the new upper storey which was then added. A new entrance gateway was opened in the curtain, and this was approached from a stone bridge over the ditch. The church, contemporary with the first phase of the castle, was separated from it by the ditch. Domestic buildings lined the curtain wall, probably workshops on the north side, and a hall and kitchen on the west. On the east side are the remains of a later structure, with a projection beyond the curtain. Bramber with its gate-house keep may be compared with the little timber castle at Penmaen in the Gower Peninsula in south Wales. It stands dramatically on a seacoast headland, and rather like Bramber the site has been separated from a gentle landward approach by a ditch, in this case cut from the rock. Excavation has disclosed a timber gate-house and a two storeyed timber hall in the bailey. It is thought that the curtain wall was of wattle, and it stood on a massive defensive bank. This gate-house was, almost inevitably, burned down, and one wonders why, with excellent building stone abundant at Penmaen it should ever have been timber built, for the land was hostile and danger must have been ever present.

Bramber Castle, as it might have appeared in the early twelfth century

1970

Totnes Castle

Totnes has already been noted as having a dry-stone foundation for its square tower. This structure was undoubtedly of eleventh century date, but the existing crenellated shell-keep is a rebuild of the early fourteenth century, though the core is probably a century older. The motte, is one of the largest in England; it is nearly circular in plan, and originally the pear-shaped inner bailey and the motte were protected by a 70 feet wide wet ditch. The bailey was also defended by a curtain wall which had superseded a palisade at an early date. The steps leading from the bailey to the summit of the motte followed the east wall—the present spiral pathway from the middle of the bailey is modern. In addition to the small keep, there were lean-to sheds lining parts of the circumference of the shell, whose wall-walk was 15 feet above courtyard level. Traces of domestic buildings and a chapel have been found in the inner bailey, where there was space and comfort—but this was late in the castle's history, when the curtain with its two towers and the wide ditch were security enough and the cramped and windy motte needed no longer to be endured.

Totnes Castle, as it might have appeared in the fourteenth century

Alan Sorrell

Restormel Castle

Restormel is another good example of the shell-keep, which, like Totnes, and unlike Windsor, Warwick and many others, did not lose its identity in a wilderness of towers and turrets, gatehouses and courtyards. Although in geography and period it is close to Totnes, Restormel has some peculiarities which demonstrate very well the flexibility of the Norman approach to castle building. The castle with its quadrangular bailey stands on a spur of high ground and the original timber shell defences were at ground level, for there was no motte. When the stone shell replaced the timber stockade the interior ground level was cut back to a depth of 6½ feet, but the appearance of a motte from the exterior was preserved by the soil thrown up from the wide flat-bottomed ditch. The wall-walk of the shell is 25 feet above the courtyard level, and there is an inner concentric wall 17 feet from the outer defensive one. Between them there was a continuous range of domestic buildings, with a large guardroom. This range had an upper storey where were the principal apartments, with store rooms at courtyard level. This is a considerable advance on Totnes where there was no inner wall, and where the courtyard buildings were disposed in a casual way, and could have been of one storey only. But there must have been certain disadvantages in the Restormel plan. With the battlements of the outer wall at least 30 feet high, living in the castle must have meant more shadow than sunshine, a gloomy enclosed habitat, removed from the world. For the fundamental difference between Totnes and Restormel was that whereas at Totnes the shell-keep was only a strong point and the living accommodation was in the open bailey, at Restormel the keep itself was the dwelling, very safe and secure, but dark and depressing too. A square tower of two storeys stood over the gate, and projecting beyond it was the drawbridge and a causeway over the ditch. The shell wall is over 8 feet thick, and that allows space for garde-robes, chimneys and staircases: an oddity, albeit a realistic one, is the loopholed latrine adjoining the gate tower. The shell wall was broken by a second square projection similar to and nearly opposite the gate tower; this was the chapel, added in the late thirteenth century when the interior accommodation was remodelled, as described above. In its later years Restormel was a royal castle and had its brief period of glory when the Black Prince, not yet embittered and broken in health by the Spanish war, or his fame tarnished by the Limoges massacre, spent Christmastide there in 1365. Then the old castle must have glowed and glittered—and perhaps all was white with snow, with its own frosty brightness. And there was the clatter and jingle and shouting of merry-making. But it was soon over and Restormel sank into decay and ruin.

Launceston is yet another variation of the shell-keep. Traces of gate towers and a stone wall surrounding the bailey survive, and there are records of extensive buildings, great hall, chapel, 'earl's chamber' which once stood there. All these have gone, but the shell-keep still stands on its high rocky natural motte. There was a low outer wall, very close to the shell wall, and within that a high round tower, thus reversing in importance the two concentric walls at Restormel. This inner tower rose 35 feet above the shell wall, and the space between was roofed over at the level of the wall-walk of the shell which was itself 30 feet high. This flat roof formed a battlemented terrace admirable for defensive purposes, and there was also a battlemented walk below the shell: so here was a very formidable three-tiered round keep, squatting toad-like on its motte, and capable of spitting venom in all directions. What is so exciting about Launceston is that, seeing it, one can look over the centuries to Henry VIII's artillery forts, so close is the likeness. Restormel, Totnes and Launceston may suffice to

Restormel Castle: the gatehouse and adjacent buildings, as they might have appeared in the fourteenth century

Alan Sorrell

demonstrate the variations of the shell-keep in its simple form where it was not submerged by later developments, but undoubtedly the culmination of Norman castle building was the rectangular keep—certainly it is so in popular esteem. In fact, it represents only one facet of Norman military architecture, and 'culmination' should not be understood to mean 'progression in time', as the following building dates show: the Tower of London, commenced before 1080; Colchester, soon after 1071; Canterbury, before 1085.

The Tower of London is so pre-eminent that we habitually refer to it as 'The Tower', or sometimes as 'The White Tower', a descriptive name which has come down through the ages as a reminder that in earlier times it was whitewashed or plastered. 'The Tower' is an all inclusive nickname, and no mention is made or expected of all the other towers, gates, curtain walls and other structure which make up the vast complex which is the Tower of London. The Tower is in a remarkable state of preservation except that the forebuilding, an essential feature of the larger rectangular keeps, has completely disappeared. It stood at the south-west corner, and gave access to the entrance doorway on the second floor, and it is probable that it was approached by way of a stone staircase parallel to but detached from the east-west wall as well as from the forebuilding. A drawbridge, operated from the latter was the only means of gaining entry. In one other respect the exterior has been altered, and the guilty person (as we should regard him today) was none other than Sir Christopher Wren, who replaced the small Norman two-light windows with the present large 'classical' ones which give the Tower its almost genial, wide eyed appearance, which must be completely at variance to its original grim look. The Hollar engraving of the mid-seventeenth century shows the forebuilding and, of course, the small windows, and the corner turrets are capped with rounded conical roofs akin to those with which we are familiar today. In the eleventh century, however, these lead-covered roofs were probably square, rising to points, similar to those surmounting the towers of Romanesque ecclesiastical buildings of that date. The walls, of ragstone and Caen ashlar, are divided into bays by wide pilaster buttresses, and spring from a wide sloping plinth, which takes account of the land falling toward the river. At the south-east angle there is a feature of extraordinary interest in the chapel apse which projects 20 feet beyond the angle of the keep: it is not unique as there is another chapel apse in the almost contemporary Colchester Castle, but is sufficiently rare and interesting because it suggests the imposition of ecclesiastical usage upon the military architects without consideration of the needs of defence, though had these same architects been able to gaze into the not distant future they might have seen in this chapel apse and the stair turret at the northern end of the eastern wall some omen of bastions and wall towers. Today, although structurally almost intact, the Tower must make far less impact on the eye and mind than when it was the dominating structure in the city and shone out like some hard white beacon for all to see and fear.

The prominence given to the chapel points to the importance of the Tower as a residence, and the planning of the interior is on a grand scale. There were originally three floors, bisected north and south by a cross wall. The western half contained three great apartments, one above the other, and the eastern half had on the lowest floor the sub-crypt of the chapel and a smaller apartment, and above that the crypt, with the chapel on the upper floor. The cross-wall was pierced by doorways and 'windows', and the kitchen was probably in the upper storey of the forebuilding. The large apartments may be called 'halls' and the smaller 'chambers', though whether that should be applied to each floor is an arguable point: certainly it is applicable to the upper floor where the Constable of the Tower lived with his family. This magnificent upper floor has a mural gallery 16 feet above floor level, and from it there was direct access to the battlements, and, of course, to the spiral stairs in the corner turrets. The mural gallery was linked with the triforium of the austerely beautiful Chapel of St John. No trace remains of the earthworks which William hastily constructed in 1067 but they may have survived into the twelfth century, and the reason for the White Tower's siting away from the river bank may be that this earlier fortification stood in the way. The old Roman city wall, repaired by Alfred the Great, was still in being in the eleventh century, and the White Tower was built close, much too close, to this ancient north-south wall, one of whose round fronted bastions was exactly opposite the chapel apse. The Roman river wall protected the keep to the south, and a stockade on the site of the later curtain wall secured it on the west and north; by 1200 a ditch had been dug along this line and the Bell Tower built. By *c.* 1270 the ditch had been widened and an outer gate built to the west, and a strong north wall with five projecting towers added, as well as an Inner Bailey to the south of the Tower, and a Water Gate. And at this time there was a great lunge to the east when the Roman wall was demolished and a new curtain and ditch made. The effect of this was that the keep now occupied a central position within the fortifications. But it was Edward I, the greatest of English castle builders, who between 1272 and 1307 completed the large scale fortification of the Tower and left it a powerful concentric fortress—not with the classical purity of form which one finds in Beaumaris, for instance, but potent enough nevertheless. Edward widened the ditch to an average of 100 feet: on the north side it became almost a chasm where the hillside sloping down to the river had to be cut into drastically. Another curtain was built and the space between it and the earlier wall became the Outer Bailey, whilst the area surrounding the Tower on the west, east and north was known as the Middle Bailey. An outer river wall was built and a great wharf pushed back the river itself, and a near impregnable barbican took the place of the old Outer Gate. The siting of the Tower of London is not ideal, by any means, and it might have gone badly for the defenders if an attack had been made with the siege engines of the later Middle Ages. But never in its long history has there been an investment or assault, and a legend of invulnerability has come into being. A clutter of residential and administrative buildings now blurs the image of the ancient castle, but they in themselves shew that it is a still living organism, and in no sense of the word a museum piece. Today tourists go in and out of what were once prison cells with gaiety and freedom, and the place of execution is a jolly place for fizzy lemonade and hamburgers: pale ghosts do not seem to obtrude themselves, and this is fortunate, for the overtones of emotion in this place could be unbearable.

Colchester Castle and the Tower of London may have been designed by the same architect, so alike are they in plan and so near in time. A comparison of the plans is instructive and surprising, for Colchester's north-south measurement is $151\frac{1}{2}$ feet against the Tower's 118 feet. The dimensions of the chapel, are however, approximately the same, and it is the chapel which links the two castles so positively. As in the Tower, Colchester's forebuilding, also on its south side, has completely disappeared. Only two storeys survive at Colchester, and it is unlikely that the third was ever added, for this was a gargantuan dream of a castle, and so it must have been quickly realised. William surely overrated the Viking menace, which in fact reached its highest point in the raid of 1071. The castle was begun soon after to combat the recurrence of such happenings, but the Viking tide was on the ebb, and the long-ships never again sailed up the Colne or the Blackwater, so Colchester Castle was left as a monument to an error of William's judgment—and William did not often miscalculate. The Tower of London and Colchester Castle stand alone: the Tower was referred to by a twelfth century chronicler as 'the fortress palace' and it has been suggested that their origin may be found in the great fortified sub-Roman palaces of the Carolingian kings of the tenth century. But whilst the Tower developed into a great concentric fortress, Colchester remained incomplete, without any substantial outworks, and though there were two baileys, one was defended only by a palisade, which, it is recorded, was destroyed by a 'violent wind' and had to be reconstructed by the sheriff. The castle was built over the vaulted substructure of the Roman Temple of Claudius whose colossal dimensions may have partly dictated the equally huge dimensions of the castle. The Tower of London and Colchester were 'hall-keeps' (as were Norwich and Castle Rising, which will be mentioned later). This means that hall and chamber were placed alongside each other, with the resultant tower having a low silhouette. The 'tower-keep' where chamber and hall were placed one above the other is an improvement on this idea in that it meant a more economical method of building and use of space—and the keep became an even more dominating structure.

Rochester Castle

The existing great stone tower-keep at Rochester stands within the bailey enclosure of the second castle to be built there. Boley Hill to the south is probably the motte of the first Norman stronghold built by William soon after the Conquest and no doubt 'boley' is a corruption of 'bailey'. Rochester, important for its river crossing on the road from Dover and Canterbury to London, was an inevitable strategic site, but it was not until 1089 that Bishop Gundulf built the second castle, and this only reluctantly after some complicated haggling between the new king, William Rufus, and Lanfranc Archbishop of Canterbury, and Gundulf bishop of Rochester. The King demanded £100 for the confirmation of certain property rights: the clerics said they had no money, and when it was suggested that Gundulf, already famous for his supervision of the building of the White Tower at London, should erect a new stone castle instead of making the money payment, this was agreed. The new castle was a replacement of the Conqueror's stronghold which had stood a siege as recently as 1088, and probably had been destroyed by the Royal forces when the defeated rebels had marched out. Bishop Odo, the King's uncle, was the rebel leader, and he was in truth, 'a turbulent priest' and far more deserving of the epithet than was Thomas à Becket. He loved war, and, debarred by his priesthood from using a sword, he wielded a mace in battle. Odo died appropriately enough on a Crusade, but with equal appropriateness he did not reach the Holy City. Gundulf's stone curtain wall enclosed a pear-shaped area with its axial-line exactly north and south in the south-western angle of the Roman city wall which it actually over-rode on the river side. The later medieval curtain stands on Gundulf's foundations: a strong bastion was added (in Richard II's time) at the north end of the axial line, a round bastion at the south end, and the wall dividing the bailey into two parts (Henry III) and the mural towers (Edward III). But all these works were subsidiary to the great keep built under a charter of Henry I by Archbishop William de Corbeil in 1127. This charter granted the Constableship to the Archbishops of Canterbury 'forever' but this surprising, and from the royal standpoint, very ill-advised act of generosity seems to have lapsed in the turmoil of John's reign (he is recorded as referring to 'our castle of Rochester') and after 1215 we hear no more of Archbishop-Constables. De Corbeil's keep may well have submerged Gundulf's keep—if there ever was one, for its siting echoes the traditional motte-and-bailey plan with the strong point pushed to the extreme edge of the fortifications, as was the case with the early, but subsequently rectified plan of the Tower of London. There must be Roman work too in its south-east wall which stands upon the ancient city wall.

The keep is 113 feet to the top of the battlements, with the corner turrets rising a further 12 feet. There were four floors, and the stone structure is so sound that it is probably true to say that if the keep could be roofed, and timbers inserted into the joist holes and floor boards relaid, it would be magnificently habitable. The plan, excluding the forebuilding, is almost exactly square, divided by a cross wall which contains a centrally placed well-shaft, and the external walls are 13 feet thick at the base, reducing to 9 feet at the top floor. The vigorous carved decoration on fireplaces, window heads and capitals shows that there was unity of feeling between Norman secular and ecclesiastical architecture. Rochester has been much besieged, and there in 1215 it was convincingly demonstrated that the tall rectangular keep was vulnerable to a weapon (if it can be so called)—the mine—which could nullify all its ponderous strength and bring its massive walls tumbling down in ruin—indeed, the weightier they were the more devastating their fall. It had long been suspected that the corner angles were the weak points of these tall towers, but it was the siege of Rochester which proved the point, and it may be said that the fallen stones of Rochester paved the way to the round tower and the concentric castle. The technique of mining was to drive a tunnel under the corner angle of the keep and then drive cross-galleries under the walls, supporting them meanwhile with timber props. The excavated space was then filled with combustibles, which in this instance included 'forty of the fattest pigs of the sort least good for eating'. Fire was then applied, and in the roaring and sizzling blaze the timber props dissolved into ashes and down came the entire corner of the keep, the fighting men swarmed in over the ruins, and after a desperate struggle were victorious. This was after two wasted months of pounding with siege engines, 'both night and day' we are told. Contemporary opinion was not slow to recognise the importance of

Rochester Castle today

the event, and a chronicler wrote 'after it few cared to put their trust in castles'. This was an exaggeration—but the invincible great square tower had become an anachronism. Significantly, after the siege, when the damaged corner was rebuilt, it took the form of a round turret, and the open-backed corner tower of the rebuilt bailey wall was also semicircular.

Rochester Castle, as it might have appeared in the later Middle Ages

Alan Sorrell

Castle Rising

Castle Rising and Norwich, both built in the mid-twelfth century, indicate a growing urbanity, a clothing of the bare bones of the structure with delicate external arcading and decorated wall surfaces. At Norwich, where the keep stands on a 40 feet high natural spur, the internal plan has lost the early simplicity and inevitability: chamber and hall have even lost their rectangular shape and are cut into by kitchen and pantry, guardroom and chapel—the last strictly confined within the square-keep plan, but with an odd corner extension which overlooks the stair to the forebuildings. What are described as 'soldiers' garde-robes' and 'knights' garde-robes' are conveniently placed and given remarkable importance. With this increased sophistication there is a thinning down of the exterior walls to a miserable seven feet in thickness, which for a keep of this size is quite untypical. Perhaps Norwich reflects a passing mood—unfounded, as the next decades were to show—of relaxed self-confidence or, perhaps, confidence that the strong government of Henry I would continue after his death. The whole character of Norwich Castle, the delightful arcading, the thinner walls, the attention paid to comfort and convenience, the whole effect is somewhat make-believe and ornamental. The keep at Castle Rising bears a strong resemblance to Norwich, they both are squat and relatively low hall-towers—at Castle Rising there are only two storeys. If it has been suggested that Norwich was a castle for peace and not war, what can be said of Castle Rising? It is not that it is beautifully decorated, inside and out—that need not be thought of as weakness or unwarlikeness, but it is the extraordinary siting of the keep which is so surprising. Imagine a great white stone dropped into a green pond, and imagine further a ripple which built up all round until it was nearly the height of the stone (the keep) and then froze, with a white crest of foam (the curtain wall), and one has some sort of picture of Castle Rising standing within its huge earthworks. No one in his right mind would build a castle in such a position, but built it was, and one can only suppose the same mood of relaxation and confidence was present here too: there is only one argument against this easy theorising, and it is that Castle Rising was built between 1140 and 1150, *during the Anarchy!* A square gateway set in the embankment survives, and there was probably a surrounding curtain wall along the top of the bank. After all the grim years past and the grim years present and to come in castle building, one can only be delighted with this glimpse of enjoyment and warm humanity when confronted with Norman Castle Rising.

The disillusionment caused by the capture of Rochester Castle in 1215 has already been referred to, but the event cannot have come altogether as a surprise to the soldiers and military architects of the day, because as early as 1166 Henry II, the Conqueror's great-grandson and the first Plantagenet King, was already experimenting at Orford with a polygonal keep with three buttresses so massive that they may be better described as towers. The forebuilding presented some difficulties, but it was fitted in compactly and with great ingenuity. Orford is a remarkable and subtle design: its flat external wall surfaces are pierced by cleverly placed arrow slits and windows so that attack from any angle could be effectively countered, and at the same time they offered only glancing targets for the attackers' missile throwers. The flat angles and the multiplicity of wall surfaces would have presented a difficult problem for the miner, who had also to cope with the massive sloping plinth. The buttresses really are akin to the projecting wall towers and bastions of the new style curtain walls which were now beginning to appear, notably at Dover, also one of Henry II's great building achievements, where the inner curtain has fine square towers projecting from it. Incidentally the enormous keep at Dover was built in 1180 and is

Castle Rising: the forebuilding of the keep, as it might have appeared about 1200

therefore later than Orford, and may be looked upon as a relapse into the old-fashioned rectangular type: perhaps Henry had doubts of his extraordinary brain-child Orford. But although Dover may have been reactionary in design, the castle viewed as a whole was certainly forward-looking in conception, with its powerful double curtain, its wall towers supporting each other, its D shaped gate towers. It possessed, like The Tower of London, many of the qualities of the concentric fortress, and what Dover lacked in science was made up for by the natural strength of its situation on the summit of a steep hill.

Orford Castle

Orford was a small castle but it was a complete and potent entity. The keep was surrounded by a curtain wall with projecting square towers which has completely disappeared (though it was intact in 1602) and a wide ditch. With a garrison of 20 men it was considered perfectly capable of maintaining itself in a possibly hostile countryside, for Orford was the only Royal stronghold in Suffolk and was in fact built by Henry to challenge the dominance of the Bigods, a family more distinguished for treachery and violence than for loyalty to its feudal overlords. Later, in 1308 it was held by ten crossbow-men and archers. These garrisons lived, not luxuriously, on a fare of bread, pork, cheese, beans and eels. Generally, those castles which were not lived in by their owners were governed by a 'constable', and there was normally a

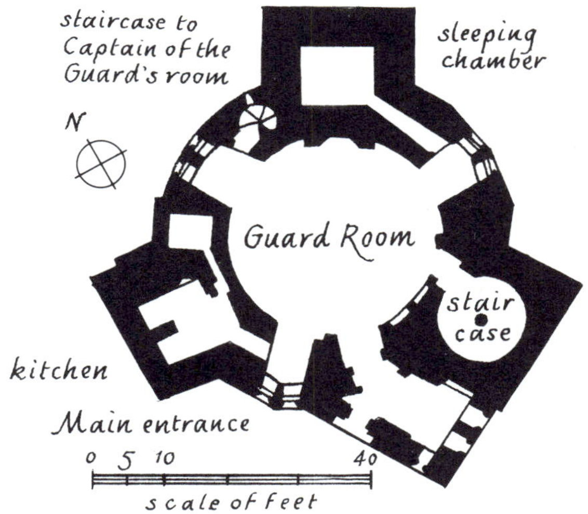

Orford Castle

← Orford Castle: the Upper Hall, as it might have appeared in the fourteenth century

chaplain who combined his religious duties with those of clerk and book-keeper. There was also the porter who looked after the gate, drawbridge and portcullis (which was invented in the early thirteenth century) and the watchman who was responsible for the stores and contents of the castle. The garrisons of the larger castles were provided by the landholders of the locality, but in later times money payments were substituted, and 'knights', that is, mounted men (not to be confused with the chivalric order of medieval times) and foot soldiers and archers were hired and paid at a fixed rate. The foot soldiers were often untrained men, who probably acted as servants and odd-job men, and were, no doubt, the stubborn last reserve in moments of crisis. The local monasteries and abbeys and priories and other ecclesiastical establishments also made their defence contributions; the Prior of Norwich, for instance, in Edward III's reign, paid £4 a year to the castle—this is later in time but is typical of the procedure which followed the change from the direct method of providing men to the system of money payments which was found to be more satisfactory to everybody concerned. Castle officials very likely preferred Flemish mercenaries of their own choosing to the short-term untrained yokels which the landholders and ecclesiastics would be able to procure for such service. The maintenance of these castle establishments was supplemented by taxes on goods coming into the towns so defended, and the English, who have never liked to be compelled to pay for their defence, frequently protested and rioted at such impositions which supported defenders who so often became their oppressors.

Conisbrough Castle

Orford is well matched as a transitional and experimental keep by Conisbrough, which was built by Hamelin Plantagenet, half-brother of Henry II, between 1180 and 1190, that is, 14 years later. These royal fancy-towers must have looked like Follies to the more conservative military men of the day, and they must have occasioned much shaking of helmet plumes and raising of soldierly eyebrows, however serious the new trends in attack may have been. There has always been a reluctance to recognise the New Weapon, and we in our own day can remember the stubborn sticking-in-of-hooves when the cavalry arm was discovered to be obsolete, and the eventual grudging change over to 'Horse Guards (Mechanised)'—surely one of the most comical of all regimental titles. Neither Orford or Conisbrough were put to the test of war so they did not prove their effectiveness or ineffectiveness, though their rather strained effort to break out of the rectangular strait-jacket does point to some realisation that the old-style tower was out of date. But it was

Conisbrough Castle, as it might have appeared in the early thirteenth century →

Alan Sorrell 1960

Conisbrough Castle today

not only the keep that was losing its omnipotence, for the powerful siege-engines which were now being increasingly used meant that the old-style curtain walls, comparatively low and thin, were now practically useless when the attack with these new weapons was pressed home. It was beginning to be realised how unsatisfactory was the situation when the weakly-defended bailey could be over-run with a minimum of effort, and the isolated keep mined and bombarded into surrender—it will be remembered that this was the pattern of the siege of Rochester Castle in 1215—and in 1216 the Dauphin Louis marched through the land with his siege train subduing 'impregnable' castles with the greatest of ease. This was a critical period in the development of the castle: the old style fortress had been shewn to be vulnerable when under attack from the new weapons, and not only were the existing structures become suspect, but the time-honoured scheme of keep and bailey was now demonstrably fallible too. At this very moment outside influences from the Mediterranean lands began to percolate through the tough shell of the Norman military mind—tough, but flexible enough to rapidly absorb these new ideas and incorporate them in his fortresses old and new. Evidently Hamelin Plantagenet had one of these receptive minds.

The curtain wall at Conisbrough, not less than the keep, is remarkable, and when it was built, unique in Britain, and much in advance of its time. It was 35 feet high and 7 feet thick and was punctuated by projecting solid semicircular towers, with widely splayed bases. Their fighting tops rose high above the wall, and though slender they presented a thickness of 17 feet of solid stone to combat any missiles that might come against them. Nothing even remotely like them had been seen in this country since the Romans had built their squat bastions at Pevensey, but these Conisbrough towers had a very un-Roman elegance, and the appearance of the castle, standing as it did upon a high hill whose sides had been artificially steepened and heightened by the digging of a deep ditch must have been extraordinarily graceful, with the white keep with its buttress towers and pointed roof shielded by the lofty wall and round towers. The enveloping landscape is still beautiful, the River Trent flowing through its curving valley and the wooded hills stretching to the horizon. Imagining Conisbrough in its prime one is irresistibly reminded of those slender white towers in the Duc de Berry's *Book of Hours*, but when those beautiful little pictures were being painted Conisbrough was entering on the last years of its active life. The keep is 95 feet high, circular in plan with six huge supporting tower buttresses, which the architect used ingeniously to contain a pigeon loft, a water cistern, guard rooms, an oven and a chapel. The two upper floors have fine fireplaces, and there are recessed wash-hand basins, garderobes and a staircase in the enormously thick wall. But lest there should be any impression of cosy comfort it should be said that, unlike Orford, it was a blind, or almost blind, tower, with so few arrow slits or windows, that not only must it have been forbiddingly gloomy, but incapable of active defence. The whole structure is faced with ashlar blocks, very finely worked and reminiscent of the craftsmanship of antiquity.

It has been said that the designer of Conisbrough aimed at making a round tower but lost his nerve, and then added the great tower buttresses to hide his shame, or to put it into other words, he could not break away entirely from the old quadrangular tradition. But other castle builders of the latter half of the twelfth century had no such inhibitions, and castles at Barnard, Buckenham, Skenfrith, Dinefwr, Bronllys, Penrice, Dolbadarn, Tretower, Longtown and Pembroke all had round towers. It is notable that there is a remarkable concentration of these cylindrical keeps in South Wales: perhaps they were inspired by the tremendous example of Earl Marshal at Pembroke, but it is equally likely that because this area was for ever in a state of warlike turmoil, the lords and commanders there required the very latest thing in fortification to meet their pressing needs. Whatever the reason, here is this crop of round towers, but by far the greatest of them all is Pembroke. It stands up boldly upon a bluff above the Pembroke River, pictorially very impressive, with a cliff edge to the north and the ground gradually falling away to the south: the shape of the bailey is roughly pentagonal. The south side is, topographically, the weakest, and here the defences are astonishingly strong: three round wall-towers, a massive two-towered gate, and a double curtain wall no less than 15 feet thick. The wall topping the northern bluff, the Inner Bailey, is very thin, but within it is the splendid circular keep: it rises sheer, without any interruption in its outer surface. It has been described as 'the finest round tower in the country'. The walls of Pembroke keep are 15 feet thick, and they are solid, without any wall chambers or pigeon loft or chapel as is the case at Conisbrough. This great structure is 53 feet in external diameter, is 80 feet high and had four storeys. At the top there are two fighting platforms, and surprisingly, a stone dome which is seven feet thick where it springs from the vertical and four feet at the crown. Evidently there was a projecting wooden gallery or hoarding surrounding the lower battlemented platform as holes for the insertion of horizontal supporting timbers still survive. The external masonry is coursed limestone rubble, and not in the same class as the exquisite ashlar at Conisbrough. Pembroke was still, in spite of its advanced type of keep, a fortress of the old order, that is, the various parts were still independent of each other and liable to be captured piecemeal. The keep is very strong, but its garrison could not seriously hinder the occupation of the outer works any more than could the old fashioned quadrangular Rochester.

Castles were a vital part of medieval life and government: each castle was at the same time an anchor of authority and a place of refuge, and it was an unfortunate fact of life that authority had many mutually hostile faces. Whether good or ill comes out of the tumult of imperious personalities struggling to prevail, or whether a strong centralised power imposing its will and bringing peace and an unchanging placidity is preferable, is something that could be debated for ever, but it is certain that the endemic strife of the Middle Ages caused this ceaseless drive towards ever more security and perfection in the castle, which was, in fact, an important expression of the age.

The energy and idealism, the rapacity, the desire to fight and conquer, the sheer inquisitiveness, and not least, the frustration induced by strong rule at home, all found their consummation in the Crusades. These folk-movements, for they were more than campaigns, had begun as early as 1096. They were formative as well as destructive, and the dark curtain that concealed the ancient world of Greece and Rome was lifted and never again fell into its old impenetrable folds. The intermingling of cultures—Greek, Arab and Western European—soon began to bear fruit in British castles with their experimental keeps, tall curtain walls and flanking towers, and an increasingly luxurious way of life also due to the eastern influence would soon affect the way of life in castles too. In a tactical way these new-style curtain walls at Conisbrough and elsewhere compelled the besieging enemy's missile throwing engines to 'keep their distance' and so their offensive power and accuracy were reduced. Not only the walls but their defenders were responsible for this alleviation, for towards the end of the twelfth century the crossbowman began to take his place as the back-bone of the defence. Slower in action than the longbow (it is said that the latter, or rather the archer behind it, was capable of shooting six arrows in a minute) the crossbow had a longer range—300 to 400 yards—as against the longbow's 220 yards, and it was a more devastating weapon: its bolt, or quarrel, caused such damage and dismay that it was condemned by the Lateran Council of 1139, but with as little effect as the later condemnation of cannon. Clearly the smaller crossbow was better adapted for use behind defences and especially in the confined space in towers and turrets than the unwieldy longbow, and a crossbowman shooting down through an arrow slit, served by a loader with a second crossbow could keep up a continuous and devastating fire. And how difficult it would be to counter such fire—to shoot upwards and through an arrow slit! It was probably not even attempted, since other methods of attack were far more promising. There was the mine (already referred to in the Rochester Castle siege) so greatly feared, but dangerous and terrifying to the unfortunate miners—and counter-miners—scraping away like moles and listening for the enemy, then perhaps breaking through into the other tunnel, and a horrible scrimmage with picks and shovels and bare hands in the flickering darkness, or the roof falls, and total extinction. There were constructional safeguards, of course: to build on rock whenever possible, and to dig a deep, wide ditch. Walls were built with a battered plinth, that is, the face of the wall inclined inward from the base (at Conisbrough the battered plinth on the curtain wall and towers projected four feet at the base and rising at an angle of, perhaps, 30 degrees joined the vertical wall nearly half-way up the tower). Fire from the flanking- (sometimes called mural-, or wall-)

towers covered the intervening straight sections of wall, and this was a considerable discouragement to mining or other operations but even so the defenders needed to be able to lean over the battlements and satisfy themselves that all was well below. But to do this would provide wonderful targets for the enemy archers, and so 'hoardings'—that is timber galleries—projecting beyond the battlements came into being: they were often roofed, and there were observation holes in the floor so that stones could be dropped or boiling pitch directed wherever necessary. Hoardings gave reasonably good protection, but a rampart of planks was never ideal, and towards the end of the fourteenth century permanent stone machicolations supplanted these additional external wall-walks, as hoardings might very well be described. Where there were no hoardings the battlements themselves were given hinged shutters which afforded some protection when partly raised for observation, as well as a shield for the wall-walk. The engines of attack differed very little from those of Roman times and earlier, and Caesar's description in the 'Gallic War' of the siege and capture of Massilia might well be of the Middle Ages, except that the Romans and the Massiliotes appear to have been more inventive and methodical in their methods of attack and defence. There always seems to have been a bucolic or farmyard trend in the naming of these devastating machines: the Roman *Onager* or wild ass became the Norman *Mangonel* or nag because of the kick-up of the rear end of the machine after the discharge of its projectile. The Ram or battering-ram was sheltered by its wheeled skin-covered penthouse which was called the Cat, or Tortoise or Sow, and the Mouse (or Bore) picked at the masonry. The Mangonel was worked on the principle of torsion: an arm was pulled back against the strain of twisted sinew or other similar substance, the projectile was placed in its cup-like free end which, when released, hurled it with great force against the target. The Trebuchet, instead of depending on torsion for its propulsive force had a very heavy counterweight at the end of the Verge or arm which carried a sling-like sack. When the verge was suddenly 'unhooked'—the term is expressive if not technically correct—the projectile sped on its way. There was a thoroughly unpleasant fashion of throwing dead donkeys and horses from these huge machines with the idea of spreading pestilence and disease in the confined space of the beseiged castle, and one can imagine the horror and disgust that these horrible missiles must have caused in a bailey crowded with terrified refugees with their pitiful belongings, and, perhaps, sheep and cattle, bleating and mooing. The thud of missiles splintering stone, fire bombs flaming like ill-omened comets across the sky and burning arrows from the ballistae all added to the dreadful noisy scene. The ballista or catapult was really an enlarged version of the crossbow—its winding-up mechanism was exactly the same. It had a low trajectory, was capable of accurate aiming and was therefore much used as an anti-personnel weapon and where targets such as wooden hoardings were within its sights.

Great movable wooden towers with drawbridges at wall-walk level were used as shooting platforms and for attack. They were known as 'belfries' and the sight of these structures, filled with fighting men being pulled up to the castle walls must have been as terrifying as the unseen mine.

This long winter between what we call the Dark Ages and the high summer of the Middle Ages was a grim period with a pervading quality of starkness which we can sense not only in the stern severity of its architecture but in every facet of life. The character of the costume, and especially the armour of the period are very suggestive of what might be called the undecorated functionalism which held sway. A typical effigy of the twelfth century shows the flat-topped round helmet, and chain mail close in round the face, and the mail shirt reaching to the knees, and mail covering the legs and feet. A long two-edged sword hung from its belt girt round the hips, a lance and a kite-shaped shield completed the equipment. But it is the extraordinary staring rigour of the faces in these effigies which is so unpleasantly impressive, and even allowing for the primitive formalism of the sculpture, it does seem that here is an expression of an age which cannot be gainsaid.

Much has been written about the effect of the Crusades upon castle building in Britain and Western Europe. At one time its importance was perhaps over-rated, but more recent opinion inclines the other way. What happened was that for the first time West Europeans came in arms against the scientific fortifications of the east and, in combat, hard lessons were driven home and learnt. It was a long apprenticeship of war and the last lessons were not learnt until 150 years had passed away. The First Crusade was put in motion in 1096, that is, exactly 30 years after the Norman Conquest. The voice which proclaimed it was that of Peter the Hermit, one of those clownish, absurdly heroic actors who from time to time tramp across the stage of history. The Crusade was blessed by Pope Urban II at the Council of Clermont on a wave of hysterical enthusiasm: 'You are soldiers of the Cross' he cried—hence, 'Crusade'. Its aim was to safeguard the pilgrims travelling to Jerusalem and the holy places in Palestine, who were increasingly tormented by the Seljuk Turks, the occupying power. The Pope not only blessed the Crusade but proclaimed the Truce of God, which solemnly condemned those private wars which in Europe had become virtually an organised trade and gave protection to women and children, merchants and husbandmen. Never had there been such a glut of sales and mortgaging of property, and buying of arms and munitions of war. The stay-at-home merchants profited greatly in all this, and probably did need special Papal protection. For good or ill, the Crusades were never organised on a national basis, and in the First Crusade only princes of secondary importance took part. It would have been quite out of character for William Rufus to wear the Cross, and it certainly would have been inexpedient for the ruler of a country still more or less under military occupation to absent himself on such a foreign adventure, but he was happy to receive Normandy in pawn from his brother Duke Robert, who went eagerly. If there was little enthusiasm in England, there was still less in Italy, which was occupied with the struggle between Pope and anti-Pope. The Spaniards were busy with their own Crusade against the Moors, and Germany showed little zeal for the Papacy which sought to humble its Emperors. But the great quadrilateral bounded by the Rhine and the Alps, the Mediterranean and the Pyrenees, the Atlantic Ocean and the English Channel, rich in fighting men with valorous and experienced leaders, some idealists, other adventurers, all burning with warlike ardour, more than compensated for any coolness in Italy or Germany. Even from Italy went the Normans of Sicily and Tarentum, all hard and seasoned warriors. The great army, so strong in fighting men but lacking a commissariat and so compelled to rob and pilfer or starve, made its way across Europe, leaving in its track the desolation we associate with the passage of a cloud of locusts, and eventually arrived before the walls of Constantinople where the leaders were charmed and humiliated by the Emperor Alexius, and transported across the Bosphorus with their followers to fight a campaign which substantially benefited the Byzantine Empire.

The impact of the tremendous Theodosian Walls upon the potential castle-builders amongst the Crusaders must have been overwhelming. If one of Kitchener's subalterns, straight from his blockhouse in the Sudan could have been transported in time and confronted with the Maginot Line, his bewilderment might have been the same. The fact that the Maginot Line failed before new weapons and because of political weakness in no way invalidates its claim to importance, any more than does the capture of Constantinople in the sieges of 1204, when in fact the land walls proved impregnable, or the final collapse in 1453 when cannon blasted a way for 200,000 Turks to overwhelm the 20,000 defending Greeks. But the Byzantine Walls can be claimed as impregnable for eight centuries as against the Maginot Line's eight years, so perhaps we should allow that the former was 100 times as effective as the latter! Imagine these walls across the landward side of the city, stretching for 4½ miles, up hill and down dale, a double line of towers based on an inner wall 40 feet high—95 great towers all boldly projecting from the wall face, square or with angled sides, each 60 feet high and spaced at intervals of 160 feet, standing on a platform 15 feet above natural ground level. On the forward edge of this platform stood another line of towers, each 30 feet high and placed so that they defended the intervals between the great towers. In front of this forward line was a second platform, on a lower level and defended by a crenellated wall, then finally a 60 feet wide water-filled ditch. This massive complex was pierced by gates and posterns, and at its southern end was the Golden Gate (which led to the Imperial triumphal way) with its two enormous flanking towers, faced with glittering white marble, with a forward work—the Lesser Golden Gate—linked by a walled courtyard, and approached by way of a wooden bridge over the wide ditch. The vital point of the whole of this Theodosian Wall system of fortification was that all the towers and all the wall sections between them were designed for mutual support: here were all the principles of the concentric fortress, albeit in linear form. The Tower of London—the White Tower with its ditch and wooden stockade—or Colchester, or similar castles in France and Flanders were not so very much larger than any one of the 95 great towers of the Theodosian Wall, so what could these northern barbarians have thought of this supreme example of scientific fortification? And yet, as the thoughtful ones must have remembered, there were in England and Wales several examples of the projecting wall tower—all Roman—at Pevensey, Portchester and London and the little

Portchester Castle today

town of Caerwent to name but a few. We have seen that at Pevensey somewhere about 1100 a remarkable keep was built, obviously strongly influenced by the nearby Roman work, and it would be interesting to know whether its D-shaped bastions were constructed before or after the crusade, but unfortunately it cannot be accurately dated. Then at Ludlow, (and in this instance we can be sure that the work ante-dated the crusade), there were built square towers projecting from the inner curtain wall, but their siting was casual and unsystematic and they were too far apart to give useful cover to each other. Even so, Ludlow is an indication of some stirring and movement in castle design, though the proper use of the new elements had not been truly grasped.

The Byzantines were Greeks, not Romans, so they were inquisitive, inventive, subject to and receptive of all sorts of influences, and it is important to remember that the Theodosian Wall did not suddenly appear, unheralded, a work of genius owing nothing to past ages. Works of genius generally do owe a good deal to highly respectable if sometimes obscure ancestors. There is the little-known Egyptian frontier fortress of Buhen in the Sudan which was mentioned above as an example of the 'hard skin' theory of fortification. Dated 1900 B.C., its likeness to fifth century A.D. Constantinople is remarkable. There is the high wall strengthened with towers standing on a platform whose forward edge is protected by a battlemented wall with half-round bastions, whose loopholes are very cunningly contrived in that they have one interior, but three exterior openings so that the defending archer had three fields of fire. There was a ditch in front of this forward wall—it was dry, of course—and its outer edge was topped by a low wall with a glacis of sand and rock sloping sharply down to the level of the desert. Buhen was destroyed in 1675 B.C. but clearly this system of mutually supporting walls and towers was in no way unique to Buhen since 1,300 years later it had proliferated so widely that it must have had many roots. It is odd that the Romans who, if not markedly inventive or imitative, were well versed in the arts of defence, did not use the concentric system, which must have been well known to them. Thus, when Aurelian built his wall round Rome (and which was later raised to a prodigious height by Maxentius), furnished though it was with splendid square towers, majestic and powerful, it stood alone. Only the great gates with their walled vantage-courts connecting them with the inner gates seemed to admit the concentric principle, but how curious it was to have limited it to only those points in that mighty 12 miles circumference. If such defences were considered suitable for the Imperial City it is unlikely that the provinces of the Western Empire would have received more subtle treatment, so the Crusaders, confronted with the Theodosian Walls, were seeing in this already ancient monument something which was to them entirely new.

Alexius, who had been quite unable to prevent the invasion of his dominions by the Army of the Cross, saw to it that it was ferried across the Bosphorus with the minimum of delay. In Asia Minor it would fight his battles, and starve and suffer and conquer so that the Byzantine Empire might live on for another 300 years. The Crusaders might never have reached the Holy Land had not the Saracens carelessly left unguarded the passes through the Taurus Mountains. Beyond the mountains lay Antioch which was defended by enormous walls in straight sections connected, or rather divided from each other by great towers, each one a self-contained fortress. Only treachery from within gained the Crusaders entry, a victory which as usual they signalised by a massacre. Strengthened by the discovery of the Holy Lance (that same lance which had pierced the side of Jesus on the Cross) they pressed on to Jerusalem. At the final assault St George, mounted on a white horse, actively assisted the attacking Christians, who, when they at last broke into the Holy City perpetrated so terrible a slaughter that their horses, as they rode up to the Mosque of Omar were knee-deep in blood. The Jews were herded into their synagogue and burnt alive, whilst Godfrey of Bouillon, the Christian leader entered the Church of the Sepulchre bare-footed and clothed in a robe of 'pure white'. It was a moment of profound emotion. Presently Saracen prisoners were set to work washing the streets and clearing away the multitude of corpses: the Triumph of the Cross was complete. Godfrey became King of Jerusalem, and a code of laws known as the Assize of Jerusalem introduced the principles of feudalism into Palestine, and since in the west castles and feudalism were so closely linked it is not surprising that a similar pattern came into being in the east, where the spreading of a net of fortresses became as vital to the preservation of the state as it had been in Norman England. But many Crusaders returned to their old homes and resumed their old lives, and in the fullness of time died and were commemorated by those grim-visaged effigies whose crossed legs were a sign of their warrior pilgrimage.

What is remarkable in the period following this triumphant First Crusade is that although Constantinople, Nicaea and Antioch must have been the subject of numberless tales, and thoughtful soldiers must have realised the implications of what they had seen, it was not until the second half of the twelfth century that Byzantine influences became apparent in English castle building. It is with something like astonishment that one recalls that Rochester keep with its weakly flowing curtain wall was built as late as 1127 despite all the ferment of the Crusade. Clearly, the tradition of the great tower and the motte-and-bailey scheme of design were too firmly established to allow the Anglo-Normans, adaptable though they may have been, to easily change their ways. But even so it was an age of

Portchester Castle, as it might have appeared in 1415

transition and experiment, and allusion has been made to Orford, Dover and Conisbrough where there is positive evidence of the seeping in of these new defensive methods. Significantly, the King led the way.

Castle building in England towards the end of the twelfth century had not the sense of urgency, nor was there the total preoccupation with the needs of war or the same need to dominate and overawe the country as there had been in the first century of Norman rule. The frontiers of Scotland and Wales were reasonably secure, and there surely was an aftermath of exhaustion from a surfeit of castles in the Anarchy. The government of Henry II was firm and energetic, though not untroubled by the ground-swell of a restless and powerful baronage: but new castles were built, perhaps as part of that long-term strategic plan which has been suggested as controlling the siting and type of castles over the whole country—and many more enlarged and embellished. It may well have been that Henry regarded Strongbow's invasion of Ireland as a heaven-sent safety-valve (or its Plantagenet equivalent), through which the steam of warlike energy spurted from 1169 onwards, to deluge the eastern half of the island with mottes-and-baileys, shell-keeps and stone towers, quite in the manner of 1066. The Irish, presumably, then began to taste some of the privileges and pleasures of civilisation, to which the Saxons had now become accustomed.

In England and Wales, meanwhile, by the strengthening and raising of the curtain walls to combat trebuchet and mangonel, keeps had been 'blanketed' and reduced in importance (though it was manifestly impossible to blanket a tower like Rochester, where Gundulf's wall gave proof of its ineffectiveness in 1215) and this strengthening of the outer defences encouraged the development of buildings in the bailey, such as halls and chapels, which would formerly have been contained in the keep. At Castle Rising, for instance, are the ruins of a substantial stone chapel with nave, aisles, chancel and apsidal sanctuary; but a large proportion of these bailey buildings were of timber construction and we are compelled to depend largely on documentary evidence for information about them. An example of the lowering of the warlike temperature of these times is to be seen at Eynsford Castle where the hall, standing in the traditional isolated position in the bailey, has taken the place of the keep. It is an oblong 45 × 30 feet, divided into unequal parts by a cross-wall: the walls were only five feet thick. It is thought to have had an upper storey, and there are ground floor loop-holes, but this travesty of a keep could not have stood any kind of siege. Even before the Anarchy this process of demoting the keep had begun, as is shown at Sherborne with its group of buildings, rectangular in plan, standing centrally in the bailey, with a very small keep in one angle of the complex. The idea of the keep being an annex and not the focal point is prophetic of the great changes to come. The keep, in fact, was losing its importance, and those who dwelt in it were moving out to where there was relatively more light and space.

But there was no peace in Jerusalem, which, with its subsidiary Christian states of Antioch, Edessa and Tripoli, established by the valour of the first Crusaders, were always on the defensive against the encircling Muslims. To counter the threat the Christians engaged upon a frenzied and prodigious castle building programme, and these same castles now standing shattered and desolate on their rocky crags, formed the basis for all subsequent fortification in Europe and elsewhere. The Crusader military architects absorbed with extraordinary speed the principles of Byzantine fortification; they developed and extended the idea of concentric lines of walls and supporting towers, and fused this mass of ancient theory and practice with the Western tradition of the great tower: the resultant amalgam was a concentration of extraordinary and unprecedented defensive power. Krak des Chevaliers is often named as the supreme example of the Crusader concentric castle, and indeed, one need not seek elsewhere for all those qualities which we see later embodied in the Edwardian fortresses. Krak stands commandingly on a rocky spur: it has no central keep, but the inner curtain which stands above a vast paved glacis or revetment, is supported by a series of enormous round-fronted towers, each one of them nearly 100 feet from front to back. There is a corner tower, in plan very like Richard I's keep at Chateau Gaillard, and a main-gate which is reached by an ascending ramp suitable for cavalry: this ramp bends back upon itself and would have been a death trap to any attacker. The outer (and lower) curtain is studded with semicircular and square flanking bastions, and has an odd, early form of machicolation which has the appearance of a concentration of garde-robes. The Western conception of the castle as a 'fortified mansion' is very marked at Krak des Chevaliers where the residential apartments are magnificent, the door and window openings delicately moulded and carved and the roofs vaulted. All this is very far from the Roman-Byzantine ideal where all was regimentation and the personal element was reduced to the minimum. It is possible to drive historical likenesses too far, but it is thought-provoking to compare Krak as it stands today with Luckenbach's excellent 'Restoration of the Castle and Palace of Tirens'. The similarity of Crusader and Mycenaen fortresses is astonishing and the time-gap between 1500 B.C. and 1200 A.D. seems to be bridged: there is the same concentration of massive towered walls, and, most interesting, in both cases the ascending ramp to the main gate might be by the same hand. It is a noteworthy example of 'leap-frogging', not conscious like the achievements of the Renaissance, but dictated by a repetition of practical needs solved by a similar intellectual reaction.

The Second Crusade was a failure, but the Third Crusade was an all-out effort by Christendom to recover the Holy City, which had fallen into the hands of the Muslims after the fatal defeat of Hattin in 1187. This time the Kings of England and France, Richard and Philip Augustus and the aged Emperor Frederick Barbarossa led their armies, and it must have seemed to the surviving Christians grimly holding on to a few coastal fortresses that with the help of these mighty potentates their kingdom would be restored and even extended. But there was no co-ordination between the German army marching down through Asia Minor and the French and English coming by sea from the west; Barbarossa was accidentally drowned, and his army, much discouraged and reduced, reached Antioch and Tyre with difficulty. Richard and Philip dallied in Sicily, and finally, Richard in sole command in Palestine, fighting brilliantly and winning all the battles, departed after achieving little more than the capture of Acre and a strip of coastline less than ten miles wide and 90 miles long from Jaffa to Tyre. Richard, bad king, bad son and bad husband, had a consuming passion for war and anything pertaining to it, and he had seen enough of crusader fortification to become inspired to build something fine and strong to compare with its best. So he built Chateau Gaillard at Les Andelys to defend his beloved Normandy against his brother-crusader Philip Augustus of France. Chateau Gaillard was a quite astonishing break with the past: it stood on a rocky spur over the Seine, and, because of the lie of the land, could only be attacked from the south-east. Here Richard put a triangular outer ward (or bailey), four round towers strengthened its two long sides and there was a fifth at its apex, 35 feet in diameter and with enormously thick walls. This advance fortification was quite independent of the main fortress with which it was linked only by a drawbridge over a dry moat. The main fortress or middle ward, whose outer wall also had boldly projecting round towers, enclosed the inner ward from which it was separated by a semi-circular moat. A highly original curtain wall surrounded this inner ward: it was very thick, and instead of wall towers, it was curved in scallops to deflect missiles. The keep took its place in an unscalloped length of wall, and it had a prow or beak very like the tower at Krak, pointing towards the only possible direction of attack. This revolutionary keep had a strongly developed system of machicolation with vertical sided arches projecting over the battered plinth, and giving protection against any attackers below. The walls of the middle and inner wards can be described as concentric, but not in the convincingly concentrated manner of Krak, for Chateau Gaillard, for all its brilliance, was weakened by a diffusion of defensive power, and in particular, the isolation of the forework was a psychological as well as a defensive error—once it had fallen the morale of the garrison of the main fortress must have been greatly shaken. In fact, a castle is something indivisible: subdue any important part of it, and unless help comes quickly it will surely fall. The siege and capture of Chateau Gaillard in 1203 lasted all through the bitter winter weather. First it was blockaded, then bombarded, and then the great apex tower was mined and the outer ward was captured. The middle ward was taken by guile—by soldiers climbing up a latrine drain and through an unwisely large chapel window, and then making such a commotion that the defenders, thinking that the whole French army was upon them, fled to the inner ward. The scalloped curtain wall was mined and breached, and as for the beaked keep, it was never tested, for the garrison sallied out and tried to cut their way through their swarming foemen. The special horror of the siege was the dreadful fate of the refugees who, turned out of the castle because of shortage of food, were denied passage through the French lines, and so were condemned to the freezing purgatory of no-man's-land. For three months they starved: they turned to cannibalism, but they died of cold and hunger and despair. The pitiful survivors were at last allowed to pass through the French lines—and died in agony after taking food. There is no trace of chivalry in this tale, it was war at its beastliest. So ended Chateau Gaillard, Richard's 'Saucy Castle'. Condensed and unified, it reappears in Conway and Caernarvon, but the isolated outer ward did not find favour though there is a misapplied notion of it at Caerphilly, and a ghost of it at Bodiam.

Framlingham Castle

Even before Richard had started on the Crusade, Framlingham Castle was being built by Hugh Bigod, Earl of Norfolk, to replace the earlier timber castle whose presence had provoked Henry II into building Orford Castle and so block access to Bigod's Flemish mercenaries who had hitherto landed there. Later, this timber Framlingham had been demolished by order of the king, but when the old earl died, full of years and dishonour, his successor Roger proceeded with what seems to have been insolent self-confidence to rebuild the defences in stone. The castle stands on a flat-topped motte surrounded by a deep ditch, with a bailey, also enclosed by a ditch on the south, west and east. To the north there is another moated enclosure known as the lower court. Framlingham Castle (the bailey and lower court need not be further

considered) is a fortified enclosure 200 feet wide from east to west, and 300 feet from north to south: it is roughly trapezoidal in plan, tapering slightly toward its north end. The curtain wall is no less than 44 feet high and 8 feet thick, and it is defended by 13 mural towers which rise a further 20 feet above the curtain. These rectangular towers project 8 feet beyond the curtain, which is in straight lengths. The main gate was incorporated in the central tower of the south-west side, and it was linked by a drawbridge with a wooden, later a stone, bridge over the moat. There was also a postern on the west side, with the prison tower on the far edge of the moat, connected to the castle by a stone bridge, and there is a further length of wall to the edge of the ditch surrounding the lower court. A similar arrangement of wall and tower connects the curtain with the northern end of this lower court ditch. It is significant that this pushing out of the main defensive area was arranged to give extra protection to the Great Hall. All this is factual and technical, but what is stimulating and exciting about Framlingham is the masterful way in which towers and walls rise high above the surrounding landscape. Here—superficially at any rate—is a translation of the Theodosian Wall, a careful, not very intelligent translation, visually like rather than intellectually profound, and the carefulness of the copy is shown by the fact that the height of the towers is almost exactly that of their Byzantine prototypes. Ten of the Framlingham towers have open backs—they were boarded above wall-walk level—and there was a continuous and uninterrupted arched passage through them—a variation on the Byzantine principle of each tower being a self-contained unit and the space between any two towers a sealed area. At Framlingham, perhaps more clearly than at any other castle, is the break in the log-jam of castle design so evident. There is no keep or central building of any kind, and hall, chapel, barracks for the garrison, kitchen and so on, are all ranged against the curtain wall. Framlingham is a revolutionary castle, but like so many revolutionary achievements it looks back rather than forward. It is a reversion to a form more ancient than the Theodosian Walls for here is refurbished the classical 'hard skin' fortification. The lessons of Byzantium had been only half-learnt, and the great fundamental principle of concentric lines of defence had not even been attempted. But with all its shortcomings Framlingham was an important breakaway, not least because it gave no privacy to the castellan. It is possible that the northern half of the castle was fenced off from the southern half, but a mutinous garrison would have made short work of such a flimsy protection. There was to be a reaction to this manifestation of democracy, and nothing could be more strictly secured than the royal apartments of Conway of little more than 70 years later. The Howard owners in Tudor days demonstrated their own particular brand of humour when they added dummy chimneys of the most elaborate design to the tops of the towers. Mary Tudor made the castle her headquarters in July 1553, when her fate was in the balance, and her supporters camped in the meadows surrounding. These were Mary's halcyon days, for here was a young woman who had emerged from the tyranny of her ogre father. She drew to herself the devotion of all these gallant gentlemen, though if they could have sniffed the reek of roasting flesh at Smithfield, their enthusiasm might have been dimmed.

That the great-tower concept was not yet outmoded is shown by the building of the octagonal keep at Odiham by King John in 1207–12. Indeed, compared with the unimpressive showing of Framlingham, which John's mercenaries captured in 1216, Odiham's defiance of Prince Louis for more than a week, in the same year, with a garrison of only three knights and ten serjeants might well have pleased the traditionalists. Odiham keep stood in a roughly rectangular bailey

Framlingham Castle: the courtyard, as it might have appeared in the thirteenth century

Alan Sorrell '60

surrounded by a wide moat, and there were two other adjacent enclosures. It is said that the floor beams radiated from a central post. Then there is Cliffords Tower at York, quatrefoil in plan and of only two storeys; as at Odiham there was a central supporting pier. Stairways and latrines were accommodated in small turrets at the intersections of the semi-circular lobes. With the gift of hindsight, the particular interest of Clifford's Tower and the rather similar keep of Pontefact Castle which they share with Launceston, is their quite extraordinary prophetic likeness to Henry VIII's artillery castles of 300 years ahead. But, in general, castlebuilding in the first three-quarters of the thirteenth century was not very imaginative or adventurous, and Barnwell, built in 1264, may be taken as a typical example: a rectangle measuring 150 by 120 feet, with strongly projecting round corner towers, and a powerful gateway with D-shaped twin towers. This gate-house is of some significance, and it shows the increasing importance given to this element of defence which was beginning to develop into the residential strong-point of the fortress. Not many years later it will finally be established as the new-style 'keep'. Two of the corner towers at Barnwell sprout eccentric semi-circular additions, one of which commands a postern. All the walls were ten feet thick, and the castle was neat, compact and strong—but hopelessly vulnerable to a determined enemy equipped with trebuchet and mangonal.

Kenilworth Castle

Walls and towers are not the only elements in fortification, and water defences, both natural and artificial, have always been important. The castle standing in the loop of a river is a commonplace, but in Britain there are two supreme instances, where the flooding of shallow valleys and their transformation into lakes by damming and other devices has conferred on them a degree of impregnability—these two great castles are Kenilworth and Caerphilly. That there is no such thing as absolute impregnability was proved when Kenilworth was compelled to surrender after a six-months siege in 1266 because of starvation and disease. The castle was Simon de Montfort's military base, and when he was defeated and killed at the Battle of Evesham his younger son Simon held it against the King—and more ominously—the Lord Edward, who later became Edward I. The garrison was in a hopeless position from the very start, but the siege dragged on from Easter till Christmas, and then the rebels marched out 'with the honours of war' (one always wonders what happened afterwards, did the defeated troops just disperse peaceably, or were they harried and destroyed in detail?). Fortunately for England, her civil wars have always been conducted with the minimum of savagery, and the siege of Kenilworth seems to have had broad farce mixed with bombardment, and gaiety with arrow shots. The attackers, unable to make physical progress, invoked spiritual aid, and brought the Archbishop of Canterbury to the lake edge whence he excommunicated the defenders who promptly produced their chaplain who, suitably arrayed, proceeded to excommunicate the Archbishop. And the defenders at night would visit the nearby villages: once Edward nearly caught them, and they had to swim to escape him. Siege engines were used by the defenders as well as by the attackers, and we are told that missiles 'frequently met and shattered each other in mid air'.

The great rectangular keep and inner curtain were built about 1160–80, and stand on a natural knoll. The existing outer curtain was probably built by King John after 1199, and it was strengthened with buttress-like bastions and towers. Henry III was also active at Kenilworth: he completed the gate leading to the causeway, and also commanded to be built new royal apartments and a chapel. Henry was more interested in what we call the 'Good Life' than in war, and wherever he went he was

Kenilworth Castle, as it might have appeared at the time of Queen Elizabeth I's visit in 1575

extravagantly partial to the amenities. In a loose and unscientific way Kenilworth may be described as a concentric castle, but its most effective fortification was the Great Pool, which with the Lower Pool covered all the west, south and south-east sides, whilst the north and north-east sides were protected by a wide, wet ditch, a man-made extension of the Great Pool. These pools (they might be more properly described as lakes) were formed by the damming of the stream which flows through the valley. This dam, a massive work 130 yards long, was topped by a double wall, and secured at both ends by towers and gates, with an extensive outwork known as The Brays covering its 'mainland' approach. That the causeway became the tiltyard very soon after the siege gives a clue to the more peaceful life of the castle that followed that tempestuous interlude. John of Gaunt turned it into a palace—but did not interfere with the keep. Kenilworth was granted to Robert Dudley in 1563 (he became Earl of Leicester in 1564) and now began the period of its greatest grandeur. Dudley spent enormous sums on the castle—he even 'modernised' the keep—and the image of the stern old castle was submerged in a flood of festivities which culminated in the never-to-be-forgotten royal visit of 1575, when was performed the incomparable pas-de-deux by the Virgin Queen and the Love-Lorn Widower, with the pale ghost of Amy Robsart upstage. Dudley laid out wonderful gardens, built the Gatehouse and set his mark on Kenilworth for ever. The purist might say that all this was 'decay' though the castle had never been so splendid, but the process was as inevitable as 'progress'. After the Civil War a certain Cromwellian Colonel Hawksworth 'slighted' the keep and breached the dam, and that was the end of Kenilworth as the great lake fortress.

It was after the pacification of the country which followed the siege of 1266 that Prince Edward left England for the Holy Land. The English nobles showed a remarkable lack of crusading zeal, and the army which landed at Acre numbered only 1,000 men. Jerusalem had long been lost to the Christians, and all that remained of the kingdom was a narrow coastal strip from Acre to Sidon. Edward could do nothing, and his efforts to enlist Mongol aid to fight the Moslems were not successful. His only recorded military action was the storming of Nazareth, and that would have been better left undone. There is no record that Edward ever saw Krak des Chevaliers, even from afar, for it had fallen to the Muslims three months before he landed, but he may have met some of the dispossessed Hospitallers, and he must have been well acquainted with the principles of East Mediterranean military architecture. Edward returned to England in 1272, and found that he was King.

Now we come to the classic age of British castles, the Edwardian Age, when it was shown that all the lessons had been learnt, when symmetry and unassailable logic took the place of asymmetry and the fortuitous. But how far was Edward personally responsible for this sudden maturity? Dr Arnold Taylor in his paper 'The Castle of St Georges-d'Esperanche' brings fascinating evidence to show how influences were brought to bear on such a man as the English king. The story is that, homeward bound from the Crusade, accompanied by many of his captains who were to become prominent in the Welsh wars, Edward stayed at St Georges-d'Esperanche with his great-uncle Count Philip of Savoy, who rendered homage to him for certain Alpine passes and towns. This improbable but well authenticated meeting took place whilst Philip was indulging his favourite hobby—which was castle building. The castle was concentric in design, and the architect and master builder was a certain Master James of St George, and Taylor is able to show from documentary and architectural data that this same Master James became Edward's master-builder and so responsible for his Welsh castles. The evidence appears to be sound, and one might therefore assume that here is proof of Edward's domination of British castle-building at that time. But there is one curious discrepancy, and that concerns Caerphilly, a superb and perfect concentric castle which the Earl of Gloucester began to build in 1267, before Edward had even left England or met his future master-builder! It would seem that like minds were converging independently towards the same solution of defence problems, and perhaps Edward, because of his pre-eminent power, and the onset of the Welsh war (without its stimulus there would have been no castles in north Wales) has more than his due credit. Edward I was in many ways an enigma: personally brave, a splendid administrator, but hard-hearted and implacably cruel, he initiated policies which, whether they failed (as in Scotland) or succeeded (as in Wales) brought only suffering and woe. He was strong enough to conquer but not great or generous enough to bring friendship and peace. And there is an odd lack of scale in his castle building programme which is disturbing, for on the one hand we are told of the wild Welsh mountaineers, and then we see fortresses so huge that they could only be taken by great armies with siege engines and all the impedimenta associated with them. True, Harlech did fall to Owen Glendower, but only through treachery, and the unfinished Caernarvon was captured and in Welsh hands for a few months in 1294—these instances no more prove the power of the mountaineers than they do the need for such massive fortifications to combat them.

Caerphilly, which forestalled Edward's castles, was built on an island, and the water of the lake surrounding it was contained by a truly gargantuan dam which formed the barbican. Three sluices regulated the flow of the water from the lake, and three towered gateways led into the barbican which measured no less than 950 feet from end to end: it was protected by a wide wet ditch and reinforced with projecting towers and buttresses. A draw-bridge connected the barbican with the concentric castle, nearly square in plan with boldly rounded corners. The inner wall had round corner towers, and there was an east and a west gateway, with a sally-port on the south side. The east gateway was the final strong-point, and was so designed that it could be defended against attacks from the inner courtyard as well as from outside. A separate island outwork defended the west side of the castle, though it must be doubtful whether it was a source of strength or weakness, since it was large in extent and not defended in a very formidable way, and it could not have been held against a determined enemy, who, once in possession, could have been a grave menace to the fortress. Its likeness to the Chateau Gaillard forework is superficial—the former might well be described as a 'weakpoint' and the latter as a 'strongpoint', however questionable its usefulness might be. The function of Caerphilly, Kidwelly, Pembroke and Chepstow, to name only the more important castles, was to dominate and guard what were known as the Welsh Marches, which through conquest and intermarriage with the families of the native chiefs had long since passed into the hands of the Anglo-Normans. But so long as the semi-independent principality of North Wales survived there was an ever-present danger of murderous raids.

Even more serious was the gleeful exploitation by the Welsh of any troubles in England, and this had occurred in the recent civil war in the reign of Henry III. It was, perhaps, unfortunate for the Welsh that the bold and ambitious Llewellyn-ap-Gruffyd had at this time united North Wales under his rule for he misjudged his strength, and dared to withhold his homage to Edward who, without more ado, proceeded to blockade Llewellyn in his cloud-wrapped hills. Soon he was compelled to surrender and do homage, and some of his fairest lands were taken from him. Intolerably provoked when Edward carved these lands up into shires on the English model, Llewellyn rebelled, as perhaps Edward intended he should, and was defeated and killed—in a nameless skirmish—and the chain of English rule was fastened on the Principality. The links in the chain were the castles.

Edward's strategy for holding North Wales was a brilliant conception: sea-power was the key to its successful working since all the castles, so diverse in design and siting, were easily accessible from the sea and so could be maintained and provisioned without the need for reliance on wagon-convoys toiling through the perilous mountain passes. With the exception of Harlech, all these castles joined on to and protected walled towns, which, filled with English colonists, effectively controlled the mountainous hinterland. They became trading centres and were, no doubt, a pacifying influence, though such iron-glove pacification cannot have been very attractive to the dispossessed sitting in their smoky cabins on the hills and watching the white sails on the sea, the gaudy pennons on the castle towers, and the knights and prosperous burghers riding by.

Flint was the first of Edward's castles, and when one considers Edward as a forward-looking, brilliantly endowed man of his day, with a profound knowledge of contemporary military architecture in the Holy Land, France and Italy, and his contact with Master James of St George, this clumsy echo of Coucy, coming after all that, is surprising and disappointing. Far from being 'forward-looking' or even 'contemporary', Flint was positively reactionary in design, an attempt to revive the great keep and nothing more than the old-fashioned motte-and-bailey done in stone—but without the motte! The square inner ward had projecting round towers at three corners, the remaining corner of the curtain was cut back in a half circle, whilst a huge round keep stood isolated at that point, accessible only by a draw-bridge. The river Dee flowed along the north and east sides, and there was an outer ward to the south, defended by a curtain wall—without towers. The plan of Flint discloses a quite remarkable awkwardness, and where a plan is awkward it is certain that the building which rises from it will suffer from the same faults. It is impossible to account for this false start to the Edwardian Age. Coucy has been mentioned as the inspiration of Flint, but apart from the difference in size (the huge donjon or keep at Coucy was 150 feet in diameter compared with Flint's 71 feet) there is a rightness of proportion and shape in the Coucy plan which is conspicuously absent from the other. The splendid Coucy donjon, after surviving practically intact for nearly 700 years was destroyed by the Germans in 1917 in an excess of cultural antipathy.

Rhuddlan Castle

Rhuddlan, which like Flint was begun in 1277, shows a definite advance in science and sophistication though, as at Flint (and at Caerphilly too), the setting out of the inner curtain is faulty. That no such errors occur in the later castles is an indication of the technical development which took place in the 18 years that separate Flint from Beaumaris. The inner ward measures 120 by 135 feet and there are boldly projecting round towers at the north and south angles. There are twin-towered gatehouses at the east and west angles, they are 40 feet in diameter and were approximately 50 feet high, divided into four storeys. Originally there were rear buildings projecting into the courtyard, thus prolonging the gate passages, but these, like all the other courtyard buildings, have completely disappeared, and we can assume, therefore that they were of timber construction, unlike similar buildings in the later Edwardian castles, which were of solid stone. The Inner Curtain wall was nine feet thick and increased to 11 feet where it met the corner towers to accommodate garde-robes and staircases, and it was 35 feet high with wide embrasures at ground level serving as arrow slits. There was an uninterrupted wall-walk, which as we have seen, was not always advantageous to the defenders—at Beaumaris, for instance, there were precautions taken to isolate the gate towers in an emergency. The differences between Rhuddlan and Beaumaris (which may be described as the ultimate in the concentric castle) are, in fact, many and interesting: the outer ward at Rhuddlan and the inner and outer curtains are at unequal distances apart, in some places 75 feet, at others 60 feet, and towards the river where the ground is steeply sloping the interval is no less than 200 feet. So it is with the great towers which nowhere come nearer than 35 feet to the outer curtain. At Beaumaris, on the other hand, the curtain walls are but 50 feet apart and the towers come within 20 feet of the outer curtain, so that an attacker in possession of the outer works would have been utterly at the mercy of the archers on the high inner wall. At Rhuddlan the relatively low and weak outer curtain with its ground level loop-holes and its small turrets was not scientifically related to the core of the fortress, and, in short, we do not see here the complete integration of the defences which is so impressively evident at the later fortresses of this period. The moat, its sides revetted in stone, was dry. The two land-gates are elaborate structures, and the river-gate is dominated by a high bastion like arrangement of walls and towers with an unscaleable battered base. In order to secure the vital link with the sea, two miles distant, the course of the River Clwyd was changed and canalised, and this major engineering feat made Rhuddlan available as Edward's base of operations, superseding Chester. The town, surprisingly—for Edward intended great things for Rhuddlan—was never walled in stone. Little now remains of Aberystwyth, also begun in 1277, but the castle is thought to have resembled Rhuddlan in form.

Work on Denbigh began in 1280. It was the castle of Henry de Lacy, Earl of Lincoln, and was built with the active support of Edward, and under the supervision of Master James of St George. The site is a dramatic one, rising high above the surrounding undulating landscape, with the town on the lower slopes and the castle dominating the whole scene. Town and castle were treated as one unit, and, as was the king's usual practice, the outer works, that is, the town walls, were commenced before anything else so that the labourers should have some protection from marauders. The D-shaped mural towers on the south and west sides of the castle with their intervening straight lengths of wall belong to this early phase, but before completion in this manner was possible, the desperate revolt of 1294 took place, and the Welsh captured town and castle. However, the English soon recaptured Denbigh, and work was resumed on the defences. This second phase was on a much grander scale than the first, and its culminating glory was its great gatehouse, one of the most extraordinary defensive structures of British military architecture. It was a powerful, self-contained fortress, a triangle of towers, reminiscent of Caernarvon in the splendid quality of its masonry and pentagonal shaping. Even as a shattered ruin this gatehouse suggests urbanity, ceremonial splendour and refinement which speak of peace as well as war. The façade, as it may be called, of the outward-facing twin

Rhuddlan Castle, as it might have appeared towards the end of the thirteenth century (above) Rhuddlan Castle today

Alan Sorrell 1963

towers, measures 80 feet across. From the draw-bridge to the innermost facet of the inner tower, the apex of the truncated triangle, is 130 feet. A vaulted octagonal central hall lies in the centre of this triangle, and from it, set at an angle to the main gateway and secured by a portcullis, was the entrance passage to the interior of the castle. There was a draw-bridge, worked on the counterpoise principle, approached by a stone ramp rising seven feet over the rock-cut moat, and there were two sets of doors and two portcullises before the central hall could be reached; 'murder holes', through which discouragement in the form of missiles or boiling pitch could be dropped on the unwelcome intruder are still visible under the archway. There was a peculiarly horrible prison dungeon below this wonderful structure, and presiding over all in a trefoil niche there is still the wreck of a seated stone figure of the king. On the opposite side of the castle are the remains of a postern gate and a barbican of remarkable maze-like ingenuity. No enemy, of course, would ever have essayed the capture of either of these gates, which might well be described as examples of over-compensation, since the gate, hitherto considered to be the weakest point in a castle here becomes the strongest: this preoccupation with the gatehouse, and its transformation into the equivalent of the keep in earlier castles is characteristic of this period. At Denbigh it becomes apparent that the designing of castles was becoming an academic exercise, where the realities of war took second place to an elaborate ritual of check and counter-check, for here no military situation could be envisaged that would call for such prodigious strength and complexity.

Conway Castle

Edward was a man of rapid action and decision, and only two months after the capture of Dolwyddlan Castle had given him command of the Conway valley, he had reached Conway from Rhuddlan. Within four days of his arrival the organisation of labour and supplies for the projected works there had already begun. The King and his Queen stayed at Conway until May 1283 and Master James of St George was left in charge of what, by any standards, was a great undertaking. Because of impeccable book-keeping and accounting we know a great deal about the day-to-day progress in building these royal castles: every detail of materials and their cost is noted—wages, carriage charges, and methods of transport, ports of origin and the names of the men who built and hewed and carved. We learn that at Conway in March and April 1283 a 'temporary wardrobe' was constructed to house the 'treasure' to pay the workmen and meet other demands. This, quite properly, seems to have been the first consideration. Money was shipped from Ireland,

and then supplies began to arrive: a cartload of iron, steel and arrows from Chester, and anchors and ships' cables, rather unexpectedly, 'were stored'. In June 1283, 20 men cleared a site in four days for the erection of a granary and water-mill, and £22 18*s* 3*d* was paid to carpenters for this job. Then there is a detailed accounting of the costs for the rebuilding of the displaced Cistercian abbey on another site, and a note that the king presented new glass windows at a cost of £7 8*s* 10*d*. Then we read that Sir Peter of Brampton on March 17 went off to Chester to recruit 200 woodcutters and 100 diggers. On March 30 Master Richard the Engineer also went to Chester to 'arrange for the purchase of tools and gear' for the cutting of rock-ditches, and for the recruitment of masons and quarry-hands and smiths. He also organised arrangements for supplies of various kinds. It is difficult to think of these transactions as being ancient and far off when we read of these supplies being sent 'carriage paid from Newcastle to Chester, whence shipment to Wales was charged separately'—more like British Railways in their most flexible, pre-nationalisation form. By November 1284 £5,819 14*s* 0*d* had been issued to Master James and John of Candover, and by the end of another year a further £3,313 1*s* 2*d* 'had been paid out', and this was increased to £11,285 11*s* 5*d* by September 1286. Details are given of

Conway Castle, as it might have appeared at the time of its completion about 1290

ALAN SORRELL 57

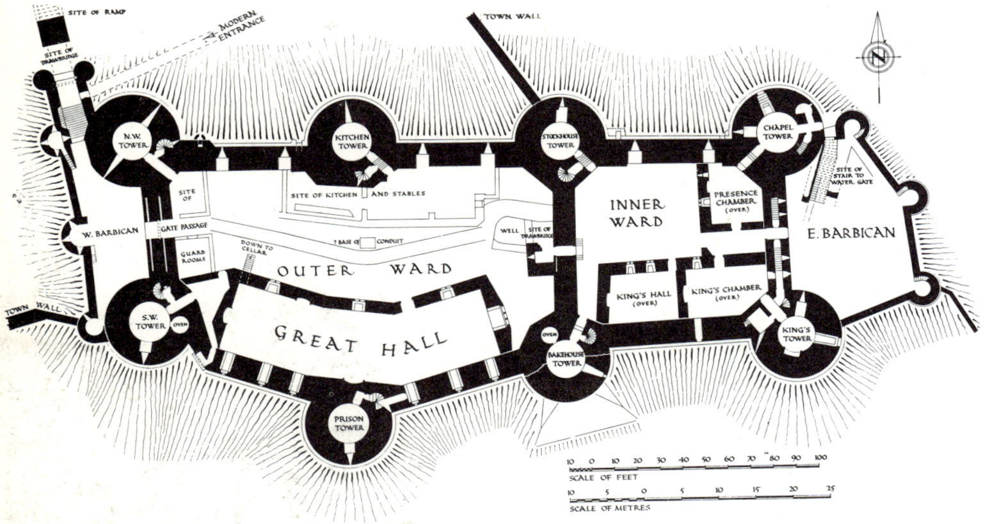

Conway Castle

'contract work': 32 sheets of lead are recorded as being 'brought in from the foundry'; Master James was paid £64 for making doorways and for 'providing corbels'. John Flauner received £8 5*s* 8*d* for making 142 arrow-slits, and he also worked 250 dressed stones at 25*s* the 100—and so the record continues. John Francis, John of Bedford, Robert Fleming, John of Sherwood, William of Launde, Robert of Frankley, masons; Henry of Chester, John of London, Nicholas of Chester, Henry de Forneys, carpenters; William Barber, Richard and Walter of Roding, William of Macclesfield and others were 'diggers'. It is a roll-call of British craftsmen, gathered from all parts of the kingdom for the king's service. We know the quantities and the cost of materials: sea-coal, lead, iron, tin, ropes, timber, scaffolding. These medieval clerks forgot nothing, and costs are recorded to the last half-penny. The overall cost of the king's Works at Conway was £14,086, expended in five years, or £2,000,000 in terms of modern currency. It should be understood that, in fact, this immense fortress and the town walls could not be built today for such a sum, even if multiplied ten times, for the skills which made them are dead.

Conway Castle is a masterpiece, and here one can only applaud in astonishment at the grandeur, power, and drama of this perfect harmony of disparate forms and textures, the smooth round towers and walls set against sharply pointed rocks with the smooth flowing river nearby. The castle stands on a long, narrow crag jutting into the River Conway, and the River Gyffin, a tributary of the Conway, guards its south flank. The town walls form a blunt triangle, whose base lies due east and west with the castle at its eastern extremity. Before the building of Telford's suspension bridge in 1826, and the tubular railway bridge in 1847 the castle had preserved its towering isolation, but now some of this quality has gone, and although the admirers of the suspension bridge may claim that its graceful curves only emphasise the solid verticality of the castle, the tubular railway bridge has no apologists, for it is destructively hideous. Now the wide new bridge for road traffic has triplicated convenience at the expense of visual drama, and Conway has lost the privilege of being a fine little town preserved from the artillery racket of the motor car. But even so the castle survives magnificently. The long north side is straight, with four round towers, boldly projecting, each 40 feet in diameter, and spaced at intervals of 55 feet. The southern side also has four similar towers, and its wall has a strong outward angle, with a tower at its blunt apex, corresponding with the outer ward and its Great Hall. The inner ward, a quadrilateral measuring 100 by 95 feet, with a wall tower at each angle, guarded the royal apartments. It could be approached only over a draw-bridge from the outer ward, or through the water gate in the east barbican, where there were stairs from the river. There is only a slight variation in the thickness of the main walls—between 10 and 12 feet, but the barbicans, east and west, with their open-backed turrets, average 4 feet in wall-thickness. The main wall-walk was uninterrupted, and whilst this meant that any threatened point could be quickly reinforced, it also shewed that the Byzantine principle of isolated strong points had been ignored: the only sop to this principle was the provision of strong doors which could have sealed off the inner ward wall-walk. The four inner ward towers are flanked by small round turrets, of no practical use, but they do indicate the core of the castle, the royal apartments, and ornament and diversify the skyline. Very soon after the completion of the castle the conical slate or shingle roofs which capped all the towers proved to be unsatisfactory in the wet and windy Welsh climate—perhaps Master James had been thinking of the more equable climate of his southern home—and lead roofs were substituted. In the Great Hall 15 massive stone arches were built to bear the extra weight of the new roof, and two of these still survive. Both Conway and Caernarvon might well be described as 'processional' in design since the visitor entering from the west end, up the ramp, over the draw-bridge, through the barbican, then the outer ward, the inner ward, east barbican and water gate, would have traversed all the principal parts of the castle, something impossible in any other fortress and it is this sheer originality in planning which is so remarkable.

On the Conway site Master George may have had no option but to abandon his concentric ideas, but no such reason can be adduced for Caernarvon, where the site is level and unrestricted. But Caernarvon had a function other than the purely defensive, for Edward intended it to be the administrative centre of the conquered province, and so the castle was given a grandiose ceremonial quality which is not to be found in the other Edwardian Welsh castles. There were other reasons, unsubstantial yet potent, for Caernarvon's special eminence, for through the medieval clangour the legionary trumpets of Imperial Rome sounded faintly but insistently, and Edward was not unwilling to found his new Imperium upon the legends of the old. Legend surrounded the name of Maxen Wledig, Magnus Maximus, who seized power in Britain and strove for the purple, and, so it was said, lay buried at Caernarvon, and when what were claimed to be his remains were discovered at Caernarvon in 1283, Edward with his usual acumen, had them reburied with great pomp. As Maximus had been defeated and executed at Aquileia near Venice the identity of the remains is unlikely, but the Imperial myth was undimmed, for was there not a marvellous old tale of Maximus coming to a land of mountains, and of a fair city and castle with 'great towers of many colours', and a throne of ivory with two golden eagles? Edward built upon this dream, and the Welsh must have wondered at its consummation by the hated destroyer of their ancient liberties. The towers of Caernarvon are polygonal and have bands of coloured stone incorporated in their structure. The Theodosian walls at Constantinople come to mind both as embodying the Imperial tradition and as the obvious precedent for the architectural form. The likeness is so remarkable that when we learn that there was in Edward's entourage a certain Sir William de Cicon, a refugee from the Latin Empire of Constantinople, it seems likely that here was a man who might well have advised the master-builders, and given them an eye-witness account of the Byzantine walls recently recaptured by the Greeks. The Imperial image was emphasised by the so-called Eagle Tower, the residence of the Justiciar, which was crowned by three turrets, each with an eagle finial. (It is said that Edward brought one of these carved Imperial birds from the nearby ruins of Roman Segontium). And the water gate of the new walled town was also known as the Golden Gate, another far-off echo of Constantinople whose matchless Porta Aurea would have for ever impressed Sir William de Cicon or anyone else who had seen it. The castle, begun in 1283 was not completed for 50 years, indeed, it never was finished, and it is ironical that this most extravagant of Edward's building conceptions should have suffered from the financial troubles which chilled the later years of his reign. The great hour-glass shaped castle enclosure measures 550 feet from east to west, and was protected by a moat on the north and east sides, and by the River Seiont on the south and west. The wall-towers are arranged with more subtlety and less appearance of brute strength than at Conway, and perhaps because of the Byzantine link, they are set astride the wall-walk, and fulfil the important classical condition that wall-towers should be self-contained fortresses. The King's and Queen's Gates are splendidly monumental and their ceremonial character is very marked. It is clear that Caernarvon, unlike Conway, was never a gleaming white fortress, and the strongly differentiated multi-coloured bands of stone were meant to be seen. It is when we come finally to Harlech and Beaumaris that the concentric fortress appears in its perfected form.

Conway Castle: the Hall, as it might have appeared about 1285

Harlech Castle

Harlech stands high up on a rocky escarpement, with sand dunes and sea below, and the mountains of Snowdonia to the north, sometimes lit by flashing sunshine but more often dark and sombre. Nobody can credit Edward or Master James with the desire to create visual drama, but, unbidden, it has come to Harlech. The four-square castle, with its deceptive appearance of simplicity (it is a highly sophisticated example of fortification), is the only stable element in the scene: everything else—flickering light, racing clouds, windswept sea and dunes—is moving. The castle is separated from its hinterland by a rock-cut moat 60 feet wide, and from this, and the levelling of the site came very conveniently a great deal of building material. The central rectangle of the castle measures 145 feet from north to south, and 180 feet from east to west. The north and south walls converge towards the west, and the east (gatehouse) wall has a very slight and subtle inward inclination towards the corner towers which project so boldly that they are almost free of the curtain. The gatehouse, the Constable's residence, is the 'keep',

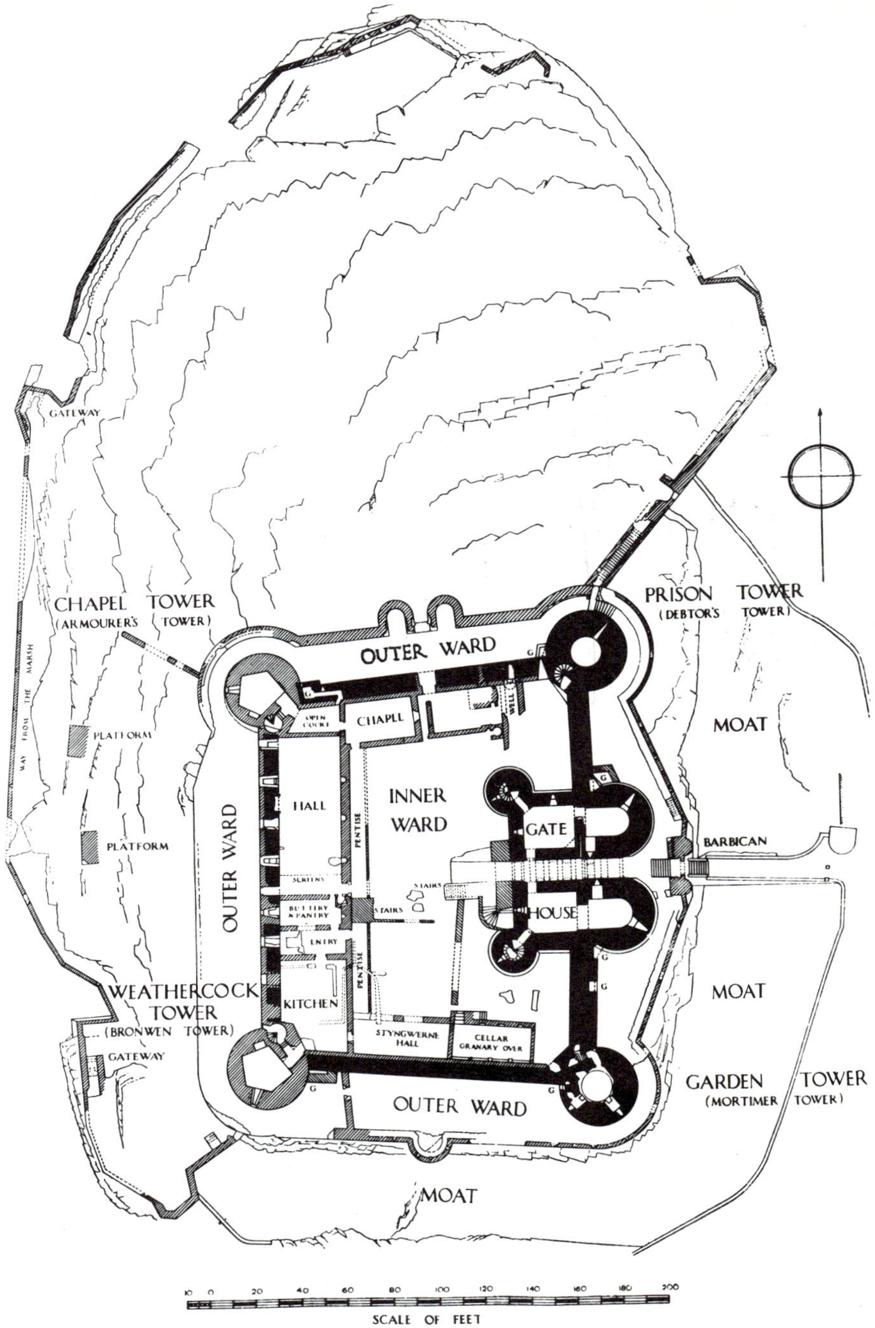

Harlech Castle, as it might have appeared at the time of its completion about 1290

with corner turrets facing into the inner ward, as well as the larger outward facing projections. Great Hall, kitchen and buttery line the west wall, and chapel, bake-house, granary and barrack buildings complete the courtyard. The relatively low outer curtain generally echoes the inner high wall, and is set very close, in some parts only 5 feet from it, and nowhere is the middle ward more than 22 feet wide. But there were disadvantages in this near-impregnable cliff-top site and the most serious was the difficult ascent from the harbour at the water's edge, (for the sea washed the foot of the cliff in medieval times). A steep path led up from the Watergate Tower, and it was defended by a loopholed and battlemented wall. In addition there were two platforms sited on the hillside, so that missiles from mangonels could give covering fire to parties humping supplies up to the castle, and a bastion and the upper gate tower (the latter was really a sally-port) gave further protection. But the problem remained, though as long as the English fleet ruled the sea it was reduced to an acceptable minimum. However, in 1404, Owen Glendower actually succeeded in capturing Harlech 'in return for a sum of money'. It is a tale of mutiny, treachery and desertion, as well as pestilence and desperation, and clearly, at this time the English were unable to revictual the castle or reinforce the garrison. Even the strongest fortress is impotent in these circumstances, and Harlech was no exception. Begun in 1286, Harlech was completed in 1290, and successfully withstood attacks by the rebellious Welsh in 1294. Evidently its design had found favour as a solution of the problem of defence for it became to a large degree the pattern for Beaumaris, which was begun in 1295, and is by common consent admitted to be the climax of Edwardian castle design.

Beaumaris Castle

The military function of Beaumaris Castle was to secure the northern end of the Menai Straits. The capture of the unfinished Caernarvon Castle at the southern end of the straits by the rebellious Welsh in 1294 must have enraged the English beyond measure, and the fact that the rebels were able to hold it for six months shows how serious the position must have been. Anglesey was overrun at that time and so when Edward had re-established his authority, the castle at Beaumaris was begun, and an extraordinary concentration of labour and material went into it: 400 masons, 2000 labourers, 30 smiths, 200 carters, and a garrison of 130 men-at-arms and archers give an indication of the royal will. That all this was a case of shutting-the-stable-door-after-the-horse-had-escaped was maybe, some sort of psychological compensation for the over-confidence that had allowed the Caernarvon disaster to happen. The

castle stands on a level site, and was surrounded by a water-filled moat whose level was regulated by a sluice. Today the castle is landlocked, but when it was built the end of the Gunner's walk, the pier-like projection which protected the dock, came down to the water's edge and the opposite side of the dock connected with the town wall. Symmetry is the prime quality of design at Beaumaris and it is remarkable that this should be so because this castle, begun so vigorously in 1295, came to a stop in 1300, was not resumed in a continuous way until 1306, and then went slowly on throughout the 1320's. Master James of St George died in 1309, so he did not live to see his masterpiece finished, but in fact Beaumaris was never finished, gatehouses and towers were left incomplete and roofless and by 1341 the state of the castle was probably not very different from what it is today. The inner ward is an almost exact square—190 by 180 feet; the curtain is 16 feet thick, the wall towers, 42 feet in diameter, are 60 feet apart, and there are two great twin-towered gatehouses opposite each other, north and south—they resemble Harlech's gatehouse, but are on a larger scale. It is

Beaumaris Castle, begun in 1295 and left unfinished in 1323, as it might have appeared if the architect's conception had been carried to completion

Alan Sorrell

interesting to compare a similar duplication in design at Caerphilly in 1267–77, and to notice the extraordinary advance in compactness and precision whilst preserving the essentials almost unaltered. The wall-walk was uninterrupted except for plank bridges which could be removed to isolate the northern gatehouse—which was the strong point of the castle and the residence of the Constable. Not only was there free circulation to all sections of the wall-walk, but a mural passage in its thickness connected all the towers and both the gatehouses. Thus Master James finally abandoned the theory of piecemeal defence in favour of flexibility: he probably decided that a defence tactic which might be dangerous on the long walls of Caernarvon might actually be of advantage to the garrison of a concentrated fortress like Beaumaris or Harlech where all points of defence are closely related. The chapel is a beautiful little chamber with vaulted roof and trefoil panelling: it is in the Chapel Tower, and originally access to it should have been from the Great Hall, but this building was never completed, and there is now a timber stair from the courtyard as well as twin doorways in the wall passage. The garde-robes are arranged in groups along the wall-walk, with another series reached from the wall passage, all discharging into the same pits. The southern gatehouse was defended by a small square barbican jutting into the outer ward, with the entrance at the side leading to the Gate-next-the-Sea, the outer gatehouse, which like the never-completed north gate was asymmetrically placed in relation to the outer curtain to make unlicensed entry the more perilous. Overall symmetry of design in the hands of Master James did not mean that pedantry could ever obscure the facts of war. This Gate-next-the-Sea must have been a truly delightful whimsy, surely not the work of Master James, but essentially English in its happy rejection of logic—though not less efficient for all that. The octagonal outer curtain had no less than 12 mural towers, excluding the gates, and it was a powerful fortification with its towers and battlemented wall-walk. Beaumaris was the last of Edward's Welsh castles and it became the prototype for many of the later castles in Britain, but like all culminating achievements, it was unapproachable, and its successors, since they could not improve upon its perfection, tended to decline both in power and beauty.

Edward did not disdain to make use of and develop the Welsh fortresses captured in the campaigns, and Criccieth was one of them. Its situation is very like that of Harlech—both castles are in sight of each other from opposite sides of Tremadoc Bay. Criccieth has two D-shaped gate towers and a hexagonal inner ward with a rectangular tower on the cliff, and later an irregularly shaped outer ward was added with two towers. A new gateway was built on the side opposite the original entrance, and was approached by so dangerous a cliff-edge path that no enemy could have reached it alive. One of the towers was known as the Engine Tower, and mounted a heavy mangonel which could have directed a plunging fire upon the beach far below to cover the landing of supplies.

Castell-y-Bere

Castell y Bere is another of these Welsh castles captured and strengthened by Edward, but it was besieged and presumably captured and destroyed by the resurgent Welsh in 1294 although the king declared that its 'safety we desire with all our heart' which is interesting, if only for the fact that it is one of the few indications we have that he did indeed possess that important physical organ. The castle occupied a rocky knoll in a fertile valley near the sea, was a long irregular enclosure, and had two characteristic apse-ended towers.

Castell-y-Bere, as it might have appeared at the end of the thirteenth century

Alan Sorrell
1961

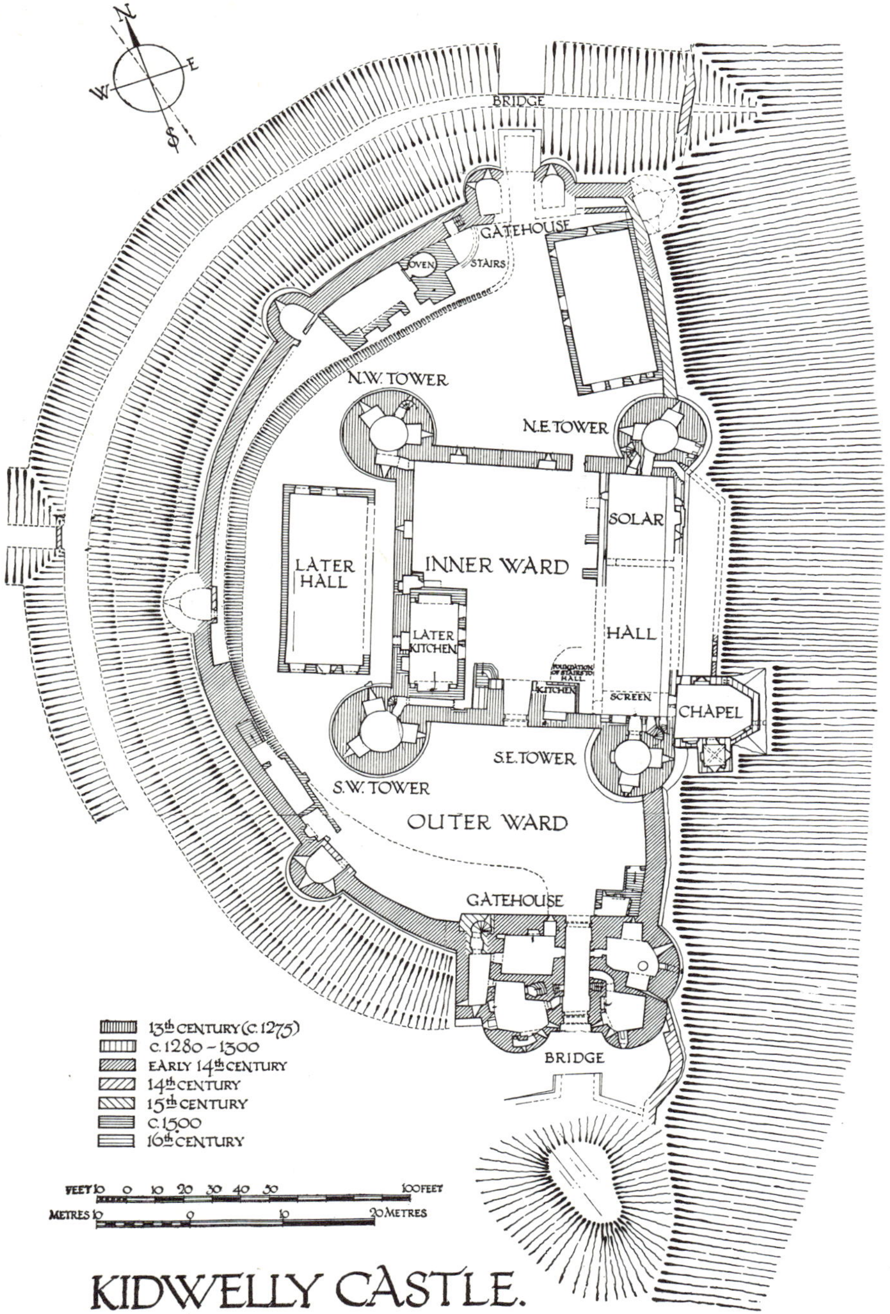

Kidwelly Castle

Rather earlier than the king's castles were Kidwelly and Carreg Cennen. Caerphilly has already been mentioned as a great baronial fortress, and it is an indication of the power and wealth of the great barons of the period that these three castles in no way suffer from comparison with the royal master-pieces. Kidwelly has an inner ward with great round towers at each corner, and there is a gatehouse which has, not unaptly, been likened to the entrance pylons of an Egyptian temple. The plan of Kidwelly is shaped like a bent bow, with the chord along the steep hillside with the river Gwendreath flowing at its foot. The bow is the outer curtain enclosing the towered inner ward and the great gatehouse where chord and bow are tied. When the outer curtain and gatehouse were built it was found that they overtopped the towers of the inner ward, which were, consequently, heightened by another storey so that they could be properly commanding. Kidwelly was a

Kidwelly Castle, as it might have appeared in 1500

concentric castle of an unusual type, adapted to the site, and the walled town which was linked to it was, in effect, an old fashioned outer ward. The town ditch, but not its wall, extended northward, curving round to join the river-side scarp, and may have enclosed a drill ground. It is odd that, with extravagant care lavished on the south side of the castle, this north side should have been comparatively neglected, especially as this was the point from which an attack would have surely come, but there never was an attack, and Kidwelly played a passive role in the throttling of free Wales, by the mere fact of its dominating a river-crossing and the road to the west.

Carreg Cennen

Carreg Cennen was a Welsh stronghold long before Edward's time, when there was a recession of Anglo-Norman power in the Welsh Marches, but it fell to the invaders in 1277, and the ruins as they exist today date from 1283 and later. The castle stands splendidly on a 300 feet high cliff-edge to the south, and with the land shelving gently to the north and east, and rather more abruptly to the west. There are considerable similarities in the siting of Carreg Cennen and Kidwelly, though the former guarded no river-crossing or road or walled town, but because of its superb defensive capabilities the site must always have attracted the castle builder—there have been finds of Roman coins which suggests a very early occupation. The most remarkable feature of the castle is the elaborate barbican in the form of a stepped ramp, which rises from the outer ward, by a right-angled turn to the twin-towered gatehouse, after passing over a series of pits crossed by draw-bridges, and under a lower and then a higher gatehouse tower known as the Prison Tower. Altogether there are five pits and draw-bridges. Rock-cut ditches protected the inner curtain with its towers and domestic buildings, and that which follows the inner side of the barbican ramp was found to have been claylined; this, together with the fact that no garde-robes discharged into it, makes it reasonably certain that here was the rainwater, that is, drinking-water supply for the garrison. Cisterns to collect rainwater from roofs and gutters have been found elsewhere in the castle, and it would appear that water supply was a serious problem at Carreg Cennen. It is always astonishing to see an immense constructional work such as this, far from any centre of population, fulfilling no important strategical purpose, owing their existence only to the fact of their inaccessibility and natural strength—one feels that here was a kind of uncouth and sullen withdrawal from the world. There is none of the symmetry and elegance of the royal castles at Carreg Cennen: the core of the castle cuts into the outer ward in a crude and arbitrary way: all is square superimposed on square, which in its prime must have created an impression of brutal power.

Carreg Cennen, as it might have appeared before it was dismantled in 1462

Alan Sorrell 1960

Goodrich Castle

Goodrich is one more baronial castle of the eastern edge of the Welsh Marches. It is three miles south of Ross, and it commanded the crossing of the river Wye and the old Roman road from Gloucester to Caerleon. It is a good example of a small Norman keep swamped and enveloped by later additions. The castle is perched on a promontory where two valleys meet, and a deep and wide moat has been carved out of the red sandstone to isolate it on the east and south. Goodrich bears a strong likeness to the slightly earlier Edwardian fortresses, as though the architect had seen Harlech, Rhuddlan or Beaumaris, and was determined to incorporate in his castle various elements which he had seen and admired in them. Thus, the gatehouse closely resembles Harlech, but because of the steeply sloping site, only *half* the Harlech complex could be included—the resultant lack of symmetry would have greatly shocked Master James, though in practical terms the solution was adequate as well as ingenious. The corner towers at Goodrich have great masonry spurs, a reminder of similar elements at Kidwelly (in this case Goodrich may have inspired Kidwelly). At ground level they become square platforms for the round towers, but they lose their significance as anti-mining devices because they are founded on solid rock, and so become merely attractive and decorative forms. Bridge and barbican are notable features at Goodrich, which, whilst undoubtedly a very powerful fortress, had a fatal weakness (not unlike Carreg Cennen) in the vulnerability of its water supply. This was cut by the Roundheads in the Civil War siege and Goodrich had to surrender.

By 1295 English rule had been firmly and finally established in Wales. The dangerous revolt of Madoc ap Llewellyn in 1294 was the last flicker of resistance, and when that was extinguished Edward could look around him as a conqueror. The country was split up into counties on the English model, and important new towns filled with English colonists, strongly walled and protected by the new castles were developing a profitable trade with the defeated people. Wales had lost its separate identity and had become amalgamated with England. The fact that the language and traditions were to survive would not have entered into Edward's calculations. But the cost of his triumph had been enormous—£10,000,000 in terms of today's currency, and that from an economy which was very much smaller and weaker than today's. So when as early as 1286 the King had turned his attention to Scottish affairs he must have realised that he was in no position to conduct his policies in a like manner. Edward's character was as subtle as it was ruthless, and, like Henry VIII he had an infinite capacity for believing in the truth and virtue of his cause, however Machiavellian his tactics may have been. His first moves were right enough, the tiger smiled. But the proposed marriage of his son, Edward of Caernarvon, and the Scottish heiress, the Maid of Norway failed to materialise when the poor little bride-to-be died untimely. Then Edward, exercising his right as suzerain, chose John Balliol as Scottish king, and very soon began to interfere in Scottish affairs to such an extent as to arouse the stern opposition of the barons who had earlier been prepared to accept an Anglo-Scottish union—for there had been no serious enmity between the two nations, and the Scots barons, Balliol and Bruce among them, had their roots in England. Affairs might have continued in a desultory way with Edward striving, through legalistic subterfuges, to gather to himself control of the Scottish state, against the stiffening opposition of the Scots. War was probably inevitable sooner or later, but in 1294 it was precipitated by a French war, Madoc's rebellion in Wales, with its reliance on help from France, and Balliol's alliance with France and his mouse-like attempt to twist the tiger's tail by sending raiding bands over the border into England. Edward reacted in a typically decisive way, crushed the Welsh revolt and then stormed into Scotland and gained complete control,

Goodrich Castle, as it might have appeared when newly completed at the end of the thirteenth century

which he retained, despite William Wallace and Robert Bruce, until his death in 1307. But although Edward might control, he could not subdue the Scots as he had the Welsh: if he could have developed a great castle-building programme in the Welsh manner—but he had exhausted his resources in Wales: if he had been a younger man able to drive his policies through to a conclusion—but he was no longer young: if he could have exploited his sea power as before—but geographical conditions were unfavourable. If all these negatives could have been positives, then, perhaps, Edward's grandiose dream might have become a reality. Against all this the unifying feudal influences, already alluded to, lent a warmer colour to Edward's hopes, and at first all went according to plan, but after the first victorious campaign and Balliol's dethronement a furious spirit of revolt took possession of the Scottish people and a formidable leader came upon the scene in William Wallace. From being a victorious advance the English campaign dwindled into a static occupation, and then it became a defence of strong points in a hostile land. Edward could not build a Conway or a Harlech for there was neither time nor money for such works, but the numerous existing Scottish castles were garrisoned by English troops. The King's positive contribution seems to have been small and confined to the digging of ditches, repairs to damaged buildings, and the construction of timber fortifications of all kinds. The scale of such works as compared with the Welsh operations may be gauged by the Jedburgh roll of four carpenters, two masons, two smiths and four ditchers, and the five carpenters, three smiths and two masons 'with a carpenter in charge' at Edinburgh. The typical Scottish castle is often thought of as a tower of simple design standing in a walled courtyard, but this is not only an over-simplification, but incorrect in a territorial sense. The tower-house concept is a northern English as well as a Scottish form which proliferated in the early fourteenth century when it became clear that the policies of Edward, the 'Hammer of the Scots' would leave a deadly harvest of hatred between the two peoples, and that border raids would follow each other in a monstrous see-saw of death and destruction into a perspective of years that had no vanishing point. These tower-houses were minor fortresses which replaced the timber and stone manor houses of the relatively peaceful pre-Edwardian days. 'Tower-house' might better express its meaning if it were reversed to 'house-tower', for whilst earlier and many contemporary fortifications should be ranked first as military or police posts with living-quarters added thereto, tower-houses were built reluctantly, to guard a family or community. There are records of dwelling houses being fortified 'against the King's enemies—the Scots'; doubtless this formula was in scores of instances reversed in favour of King Robert Bruce. Some of these refuges may now be called castles though originally the towers stood alone, as at Craigmillar in Midlothian, where the courtyard and surrounding buildings, and the curtain wall with its round corner turrets were not added until 1427—50 years later—a sure sign of the increasing state of anarchy.

Threave Castle, on an island in the River Dee near Dumfries, was built in 1380, and is a tall oblong tower set in a walled enclosure with open-backed corner turrets. The tower had a two-storeyed kitchen in the basement, and there were three storeys above, all reached by a spiral stair. Threave tower could only be entered by climbing up a ladder to a door on the second storey, though there was also a postern escape route from the third floor by way of a wooden bridge to the gate of the outer wall, from which it would seem that acrobatic skill was vital to survival in those troubled times. Fire places, latrines, a stone sink, a well, and even a small windowless prison were among the amenities. The walls were 8 feet thick at the base, and the rooms measured 24 by 47 feet, and some of them, because of their size, were probably sub-divided. The fighting deck was protected by battlements, and three of the interior wall-faces are pitted with small square holes which are supposed to have housed a colony of pigeons, though why Archibald the Grim who built Threave should have provided accommodation for pigeons has never been discovered. Threave was one of the larger tower houses, and living in it may have been bearable, but in the smaller towers, and especially the so-called *pele* towers of a slightly later date, the congestion and stench and fear must have been intolerable. On the one hand there was the craving for safety, and on the other the desire for comfort and the normal amenities of life. This stress between two objectives was never satisfactorily resolved in architectural form, and it may be that the highly picturesque silhouettes sometimes achieved, of turrets supported on corbels, with snuffer roofs, and chimneys, gables and battlements, were attempts to express the domestic, as opposed to the warlike uses of these tower-houses.

Caerlaverock Castle

Edward's successful aggression in Wales led to the construction of the most up-to-date fortresses in western Europe: his unsuccessful aggression in Scotland led to a reversion in fortification to a type of castle that had become out-of-date 150 years before. But there were also in Scotland some castles of great splendour and originality, and Caerlaverock is in the second category. It is triangular in plan, and

Caerlaverock Castle, as it might have appeared in the fifteenth century

faces north. This is important and suggests that its inspiration was English rather than Scottish, and that, standing as it did on the northern shore of the Solway Firth, Caerlaverock was intended as a bridgehead for the invader from the south. There are still visible the remains of an older castle closer to the seashore, which appears to have been set on an artificial island with a sheltered harbour, and a dyke or sea-wall connects this with the 'new' castle which stands surrounded by a wide water-filled moat. There is only one entrance, from the north, where the moat narrows, and was once spanned by a wooden bridge secured at both ends by draw-bridges which lead directly into the twin-towered gatehouse, the strong-point of the castle and the apex of its triangular plan. So exact is the geometry of the equilateral triangle with its gatehouse apex and its other angles each terminated by a round tower, that if the sides of the triangle are extended it will be found that their junctions are in the true centres of these towers. With Caerlaverock we come to the 'picturesque' in castle architecture. We have had martial austerity, then lucid grandeur, and now the picturesque. The craving for the decorated silhouette has already been mentioned, and here it became a rich tangled jungle growth of corbelled corner turrets, machicolated and battlemented parapets, chimneys and pointed roofs and gables, wooden hoardings surmounting the curtain wall, and fluttering banners and gilded finials. Perhaps, too, there was a French influence, and the Duc de Berry's *Book of Hours* will be remembered. The visual harmony-by-contrast between this complicated and eccentric sky line and the long horizontals of the flat lands bordering the Solway and the sea beyond to the English shore show a rare intuitive sensitiveness to shape and form, which had nothing to do with the necessities of fortification. Inside the castle, on the east flank of the courtyard, is a Renaissance fantasy known as Nithsdale's Apartments, added when it was mistakenly thought that wars and sieges would never come again, and that it was time to play. But Caerlaverock was 'slighted' in the Civil War, and became the romantic ruin that so took the fancy of Sir Walter Scott that he made it the centrepiece for 'Guy Mannering'.

Bothwell Castle

If Caerlaverock had picturesqueness Bothwell had splendour as its prime visual quality, for it recalls Coucy, Najac, and Flint—of which, built in 1277, it was the exact contemporary. Coucy and Najac were built between 1225 and 1250, and the possibility that here too there was French influence is increased by the perfection of the polished ashlar masonry, something far beyond the capacity of Scottish craftsmen of that time.

(top left) Caerlaverock Castle today; (above) Bothwell Castle today

Bothwell Castle, as it might have been completed in the thirteenth century

Alan Sorrell 1959

The plan is simply an oblong inner bailey with projecting round and square towers and an enormous round keep or donjon at its western end. This donjon was nearly 70 feet in diameter and was perhaps 90 feet in height, and the adjacent curtain walls were not less than 60 feet high. The short diagonal curtain ends in the round Prison Tower, and there is an elaborate arrangement of latrines, corbelled out, all of the most beautiful and ingenious construction, and there was an arrangement to flush the latrine pit from the rock-cut ditch which divided the donjon from the rest of the castle. This degree of sophistication points to an intelligence which Master James would have recognised. To the north there are substantial foundations of a gatehouse, towers and curtain to enclose a roughly triangular outer bailey. These were never finished, but even in its incompleteness Bothwell was a very grand castle. It was never a fortunate castle and its history is a confusion of building, intended building, demolition and partial rebuilding.

The donjon, which could only be approached from the inner bailey by a draw-bridge over the rock-ditch, had four storeys with wooden floors, the first and second supported on an octagonal stone pier from which sprang, diagonally, low stone arches. The top floor was the lord's private apartment or *camera* with its own covered way leading to the wall-walk and the Prison Tower and its postern, an escape route for use in an emergency. It is reasonable to think that there was a low outer loopholed wall with a postern gate and a path down the steep slope to the river Clyde. Edward captured Bothwell after a siege of less than a month in September 1301. He had an army of 6,800 men, but his most impressive weapon appears to have been a giant siege-engine, a wooden tower of several storeys, a 'belfrey' which had a draw-bridge at the top, and this, when it was lowered on to the wall-walk of its victim-castle, disgorged a stream of armed men. This belfrey was constructed in Glasgow, and it was dragged along the rough track to Bothwell, eight miles away, in two days. Then a bridge over the Clyde was built (to provide the timber for it the 'wood of Glasgu' was despoiled), and finally a corduroy road was made so that the monster could be wheeled right up to the castle walls.

Edward was a strange man, with his values inextricably mixed, for we learn that in addition to his belfrey, he had his portable chapel which, carried on a wagon drawn by two oxen, went with him on all his military expeditions. On this occasion, after the army had 'received an instalment of pay' Edward piously made 'an oblation of seven shillings in honour of the Virgin in his field-chapel', and the attack began.

Dirleton Castle

Dirleton was another important Scottish castle of sternly romantic appearance, standing on a crag where the land slopes down to the grey waters of the Firth of Forth, a mile away. The building periods extend from the thirteenth to the sixteenth centuries. Basically, the plan is an obtusely angled L-shape, with four part-round towers ranged along the two arms and the curtain wall, raised on the almost vertical crag completing the fortified area. The wooden-bridge over the 70-foot-wide ditch rose 12 feet to a draw-bridge fronting the tall and narrow entrance archway—it was 18 feet high, and very similar to the archway at Caerlaverock. Two small corbelled snuffer-roofed turrets were high up, flanking this entrance with its drawbridge-pit (later filled in) and supporting round towers. Compared with Caerlaverock and Bothwell it is all strangely out of balance. However, the site is a strong one, and the quarrying of building stone from the west face of the crag added 20 feet to the curtain, so that the vertical height of the defences totalled 40 feet. At Dirleton there is no breath of the mathematical precision and logic of the Edwardian fortresses, and like so many castles its strength was like that of a muscle-bound heavyweight prizefighter.

Dirleton Castle, as it might have appeared in the early fourteenth century

Following the brilliant Edwardian castle building period there came a reaction to something like somnolence. Except for the chronic state of intermittent warfare in the north there was relative peace in England, though the mere fact that castles were still being built shows that security was far from being regarded as normality. The onset of the Hundred Years War meant that the fighting men, the potentially troublesome barons and their retainers crossed the Channel—and when they returned, sated with rapine and slaughter, they brought with them the plunder of France. Amenity and comfort now became the foremost considerations in British castle building, though the fundamental military requirements were by no means neglected.

Maxstoke in Warwickshire, built in 1345, may be regarded as a fair example of the rational, dull, tolerably efficient and convenient residential castles of the period. Square in plan with octagonal corner towers and a projecting gatehouse with all the warlike appurtenances, draw-bridge, portcullis, and even 'murder holes'. Domestic buildings lined the curtain wall opposite the gatehouse, and it was originally intended that three sides should be so lined. Maxstoke is protected by a wet moat, which contradicts the feeling of spacious serenity and peace.

Bolton Castle is more concentrated, with its high walls and square corner towers. Domestic buildings entirely enclose the courtyard which could only be entered from gateways in the corners, and the main gate: all were closed by portcullises, so here we have a different kind of concentric castle where the enemy could be trapped in the courtyard instead of between two lines of walls.

A castle more in the true line of Beaumaris is Bodiam, built between 1386 and 1390, specifically for defence against possible French invaders—for the war ebbed and flowed. It still stands beautifully in its lake—for it would be impertinent to call a piece of water measuring more than 550 feet by 300 feet a 'moat'. It is difficult to treat Bodiam in an objective way, for it has been bombarded with every imaginable cliché. Even Lord Curzon who left it to the nation described it as 'the most romantic and fairy of English castles'. Nevertheless, Bodiam was a strong implement of war—a high curtain wall, alternating round and square towers, a fine machicolated gatehouse and postern, and a particularly ingenious barbican and outwork with wooden bridges and draw-bridges at right-angles to each other, all these contributed to a defensive potential not in the least 'fairy'. The two-storeyed domestic buildings were ranged around all four sides of the courtyard, and we might pause to notice the absence of outer ward and any easily recognisable keep or strongpoint. Herstmonceaux is of slightly later date (*c.* 1440) and it demonstrates a further stage in the decline of the castle as a fortification. Although it has all the formal requisites of a fortress—octagonal wall towers, gatehouse, draw-bridge and so on, it was a play castle, built by a tired old soldier to remind him of battles long ago, but battles no longer dangerous or vicious when seen against this background of red rose brick and reflected in the still water of the moat, water-lilies, sailing swans and all. Herstmonceaux was—and is—a stately castle, but the day of the stately castle was nearly over, for the great climacteric had come in the form of the bulbous iron-bound tube—the cannon. As early as 1327 cannon had been used against the Scots, and at Crecy in 1346 they had added their voice to the cacophony of battle. The first cannon probably caused as much damage to those who operated them as to their opponents, but the engineers saw clearly enough their future as long-range battering-rams, and their development was rapid. By altering their elevation cannon became mortars, and outclassed the trebuchet. The new weapon was used to great effect by the French, and a cynical but, perhaps, perceptive historian has declared that the cannon had more to do with driving the English out of France than Jeanne d'Arc. It is certainly true that the Constable Bertrand de Gueschlin captured 60 English-held castles by the skilful use of his siege artillery in the course of a year's campaigning. The immortal breach at Harfleur was the result of Henry v's cannonade, although in that instance and no doubt in others too, the older weapons, mangonel and trebuchet, were ranged alongside the new. Even the mighty walls of Constantinople were not exempt from the downfall, and Turkish cannon blasted a way through them in 1453. Not only was the new style cannonade a dangerous threat, but the mounting of counter batteries on the walls and towers was often more destructive to their fabric than the bombardment itself, and this was so at Constantinople where the ancient towers simply could not survive the shock and vibration of their own artillery.

Up to the time of the Wars of the Roses—the mid-fifteenth century—cannon bombardment must have seemed a remote contingency to the castle dweller in England: castles were not only becoming more luxurious, but there was a growing desire by the lordly families for apartments entirely separate from their garrisons. The great Edwardian gatehouses are held to be early examples of this desire for privacy and security, but they were so linked with critical defensive requirements that they could not be thought of as being really suitable. The Eagle Tower at Caernarvon, the residence of the Justiciar, and the most splendid tower in the castle, is nearer to the ideal: it was in a comparatively secure defensive position, it was a self-contained fortress, and it had a postern escape route—all important qualifications for the new style residential tower-houses which were to come.

The Scottish and Border tower-houses have already been referred to, but their function was totally different from the lordly tower-houses of the south and midlands: the former were directed against attack from without and their defensive capabilities were far in excess of their capacity for amenity, whilst the latter had privacy and luxury of a much higher priority than security, important though that may have been on the probably rare occasion of a mutinous garrison attempting to assault the lord and his family. There were many Continental tower-houses, French, Spanish, German and Italian, and quite obviously this desire for luxury and privacy was by no means an exclusively English trend. Some authorities see a foreign influence at work in England, but it seems more likely that these sophisticated nobles of the fourteenth century looked nostalgically at those great old Norman keeps which still stood in their antique grandeur in all parts of the country, and decided that here was the form which, suitably decorated and civilised, and built in materials which could not be confused with the Norman originals, would suit their purpose very well.

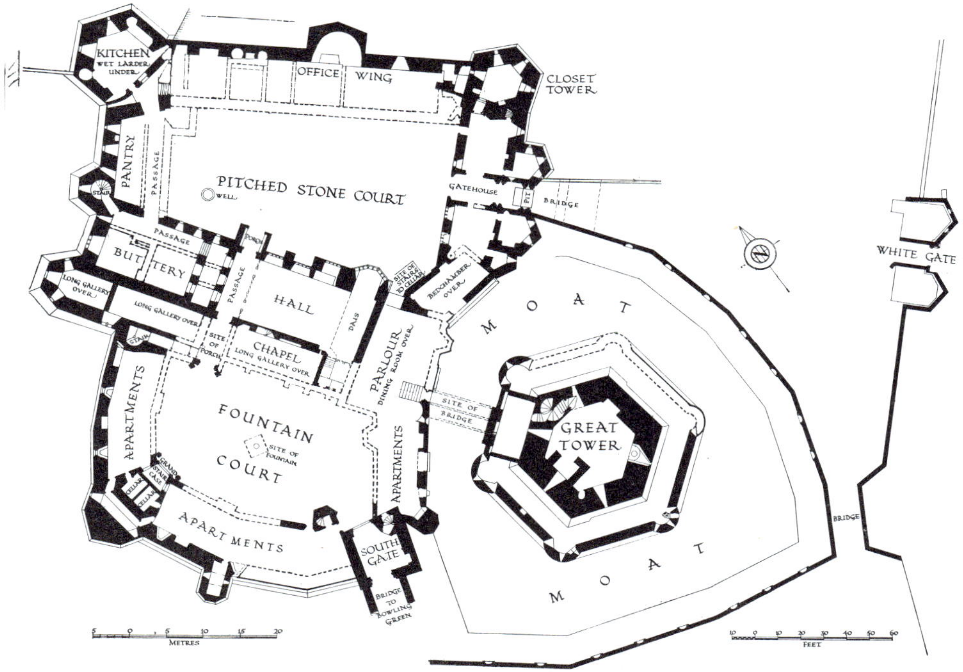

It was an exercise in antiquarianism, not Victorian Gothic, but Plantagenet Norman. At Tattershall there is a splendid tower-house built in 1433, standing out beyond the thirteenth century curtain wall of the inner bailey. It is 100 feet high to the top of the parapet, and 120 feet to the top of the corner turrets. To make its formal likeness to the Norman keep even closer there was actually a forebuilding! A wide spiral staircase leads to the upper floors, and at the summit there are battlements and machicolations—defence was not neglected, though the large traceried windows and the weakly-defended entrance show that peace rather than war was the governing principle at Tattershall. Nevertheless, that these new style ornamental keeps were formidable structures even in the age of cannon is confirmed by a report of the Parliamentary Commissioners in 1648: 'We are likewise informed that the Great Tower of Ashby-de-la-Zouch' is 'a place of considerable strength'. On this report orders were made for the tower to be slighted—which was done. Ashby and all the other castles of the period had gun-ports, and these were not always designed with a very clear understanding of the new weapons—sometimes they were placed for effect rather than use, as the Civil War defenders must have found to their cost.

Raglan Castle

Raglan, even in decay still grandiose and splendid, was one of the screen of castles guarding the Welsh Marches. It was of early foundation but the ruins which survive today are of the fifteenth century and later. The superb tower, the Yellow Tower of Gwent, is not only a marvel but is a puzzle too. One asks why, at that time, when the danger of Welsh uprising and raids had gone for ever, this extravagant folly (which makes William Beckford's Fonthill look like the tinkering of a peculiarly foolish child), should ever have been built. For Raglan does not fit into any category: it is too massive and formidable in conception to be classed with Tattershall and the other make-believe keeps of the period, and yet the style of its construction has a crazy pointlessness which only attains some sort of reason when it can be thought of as a symbol of the arrival of a 'new man', in this instance Sir William ap Thomas, a soldier of the French wars, a country squire who married first, Elizabeth 'the lady of Raggeland' and second, the heiress of the Vaughans. Both these ladies were of high birth and through their wealth ap Thomas became a power in the land, and he built the Yellow Tower to show to the world his new nobility and importance—that he chose to do so in the super-grand manner bears the hallmark of the typical *parvenu.* No doubt there was lawlessness at this time, with other war veterans, not so fortunate as ap Thomas, ready for any kind of violence, but his tower was ridiculously huge if it was only intended to preserve his privacy and protect his family from mutinous mercenaries and wandering bands of violent men. The Yellow Tower was built on what was probably the core of the early Norman motte, and the two courtyards, sloping down the hillside to north and west, echo the shape of the old Outer Bailey. The tower is octagonal in plan on a battered base, and its walls have a pronounced inward slope. The base diameter is 60 feet and its full height, including machicolations and battlements must have been over 100 feet. There were five storeys each with one large room, and a wide newel-stair gave access to them all. The base of the tower was supported by a walled terrace which may have mounted light cannon, and it was surrounded by a wet moat on whose revetted outer edge was another terrace ornamented with wall niches and adorned with 'several figures of the Roman Emperors in arches of divers varieties of shell-work'. At Raglan the High Renaissance cannot be divorced from the Middle Ages, it is all mixed up into a most glorious hodge-podge.

Beyond the terrace was the bowling green where Charles I played in 1645, and his dwarfish bandy-legged figure silhouetted against the afternoon sun can be readily imagined. Physically insignificant though he may have been, he was the harbinger of destruction for all this accumulation of power and fancy.

A weak outer curtain wall was built in the early seventeenth century with the White Gate as a protection for the Great Gate (this was toying with fortification) and further out still another wall with a Red Gate was begun but never completed. There were two gateways, the Great Gatehouse to the north of the Tower, the other to the south; the former led into the Pitched Stone Court, the latter into the parallel Fountain Court where stood 'a pleasant marble fountain in the midst thereof called the White Horse, continually running with a clear water'. The main group of residential buildings divided the two courts and included hall, parlour, dining room, chapel, long gallery and buttery. These were connected to the tower by a 'sumptuous arched bridge' which gave entry at first-floor level. The two courts were surrounded by apartments of two storeys, the upper floor served by the Grand Staircase in the Fountain Court. Raglan was a group of structures of the utmost complexity, made possible by the enormous wealth of its owners which they delighted to lavish on its extension and decoration, and it illustrates very well the final glorification and degeneracy of the medieval castle. Strong it was, as the Parliament army was to find, but if this style of luxurious living was desired, then it might have been better to divorce it completely from this exaggerated military setting with its strong towers and gun-ports and draw-bridges. The paradox is that if this palace had been less of a castle it might well have escaped its quite inappropriate fate, the final irony of the siege—surely of all contingencies the least expected. So far removed from the grim realities of Harlech and Conway, with its orchards and parks and great fishponds 'ornamented with divers artificial islands and walks', Raglan suffered from its defensive insufficiences, as the unfortunate Marquis of Worcester found to his cost: he 'had to dine in his withdrawing-room to the accompaniment of musket balls coming in through the windows'. Even so Raglan manfully withstood the spoiling bombardment until the hopelessness of the Royal cause made surrender inevitable. The fall of Raglan was much more than an episode in the Civil War, it was the end of an age, and it is significant that, although after the Restoration wealth abundant remained with the family, the grandson of the Marquis, created Duke of Beaufort, rather than repair the castle, chose to build a great mansion at Badminton where there was no pretence whatsoever to fortification.

By the late fifteenth century castles all over the country were entering into this state of opulent degeneracy of which Raglan is the prime example. Kenilworth, already a palace, was further embellished by the Earl of Leicester in the second half of the sixteenth century, who made it

Raglan Castle, as it might have appeared at the time of King Charles I's visit in 1645

the perfect backcloth for his Elizabethan frolics. His Great Gate-House, splendid though it may be, is a travesty of its stern predecessors, and the fragility of the so-called Leicester's Buildings indicate very clearly that the long tug-of-war between fortress and residence was nearly over.

Helmsley Castle

Helmsley Castle, in Yorkshire, is a good example of changing conditions, and is more typical than either Raglan or Kenilworth, which were the products of almost unlimited wealth and power. The keep is *c.* 1190, D-shaped and projecting beyond the curtain. The quadrilateral of the castle is enclosed by two ditches and embankments, the outer topped by a wooden palisade. There was a strongly-defended Barbican at the south-east end, with walls spanning the inner ditch, and an Outer Gate with half-round twin-towers of the thirteenth century, but refaced in the Renaissance manner in the late sixteenth century. There is evidence that the gate towers, corner towers and intervening wall were furnished with wooden hoardings. Stone and timber bridges spanned outer and inner ditches, and the Inner Gate-House was early in date, as were the foundations of the domestic buildings which were erected in the sixteenth century. In addition to the Barbican at the south-east end of the castle, there was a strong gate with half-round towers, and an outer work at the opposite end, where the curtain also had half-round corner towers. It can be claimed that Helmsley was a concentric castle, but compared with the close knit, passionate precision of Beaumaris it was a poor thing. Certainly the degeneracy of Helmsley cannot be described as 'opulent' but the change in emphasis from war to peace is very marked, for the domestic buildings were large in scale, and were no doubt the scene of a rich and generous social life, far enough from London to have provincial independence, and yet near enough to be fully aware of events, cultural and political.

Bolsover Castle

Bolsover was an early Pennine fortress, with two baileys and a great square keep, but the Cavendishes built a stately mansion over it in the second decade of the seventeenth century. Now the mansion is roofless and derelict, and, from its steep hillside looks over a land as derelict and devastated as itself.

But before these late developments, Henry VIII had built his artillery forts along the south coast in the first part of the sixteenth century. From the tower-house to these forts there is a prodigious descent if one thinks in a vertical way, but in time only 100 years separated them. It was a revolution—a genuine revolution, a complete turn of the wheel back to the primitive purely military type of fortification. There is nothing of the 'fortified mansion' in Henry's artillery forts which came into being because of the changed political conditions of the times, no less than the increasing domination of the cannon. In 1538 no longer 'fair stood the wind for France' for the wind-of-war blew strongly towards England, and it was constant for almost exactly 150 years. It became a tempest in 1588, and was scarcely less dangerous in 1666 when the Dutch sailed up the Thames and blockaded London itself. In 1538 the long-nosed Valois, Francis of France, and the Emperor Charles with his great Hapsburg under-lip, agreed to a truce, grudgingly enough, for ten years, and against a background of Papal fulminations (Henry was compared with the Turk, which was flattering rather than otherwise to the gross Tudor, mean-mouthed and porcine, for the 'Turk' at that time was Suleyman the Magnificent), England prepared to meet the threatened invasion. Henry's castle building programme was a very extensive one, and although the more important castles, forts or the smaller 'bulwarks' were sited along the south coast and the Thames estuary—other parts of the kingdom, the frontier of Scotland and even the Isle of Man were not neglected. No such systematic castle building had been seen in Britain since Edward's day, but whereas Edward built to dominate, Henry built to defend. The Plantagenet scheme was localised

Helmsley Castle, as it might have appeared about 1500

Alan Sorrell 1963.

Bolsover Castle: the Earl of Newcastle's state rooms, as they were about 1640

but grandiose, the Tudor was national, and—in every sense of the words—down to earth. These artillery forts, small, squat, symmetrical in plan, expressing as they do recognition of the powerful new weapon, may have been influenced by Italian designers of the Quinquecento. Italian commanders had been appalled by the easy conquest of their castles by the French invaders in the last years of the fifteenth century and they realised that radical changes in design were necessary. Their new ideas to cope with the menace were quite logical. Since cannon balls could batter walls so disturbingly, obviously it would be advantageous to the defence to offer smaller targets, therefore no more tall towers or curtains, and since the impact of the cannon ball could be reduced if only glancing blows were possible, therefore, reasoned the experts who were responsible for Henry's forts, let us have curved surfaces everywhere, so that the direct shattering blow becomes almost an impossibility. But one feels that the gifted designers and draughtsmen, poring over their drawing boards, were seduced by the sheer abstract beauty of their interlocking circles and cloverleaf patterns and forgot the grim practicalities of bombardment. They forget or ignored what any small boy knows, that a ball—whether a play-ball or a cannon-ball—trapped in the intersections of these interlocking walls would richochet in a devastating way. And they could only visualise castles built of stone, with vertical walls, and, unfortunately, stone splinters under bombardment inflict terrible wounds and cause widespread destruction. Only a sloping earth glacis could absorb and nullify the shock of the cannon ball. Probably the long tradition of high unclimbable stone walls could not be easily discarded and the earthen banks were not to come for a century. But perhaps the designers' vital error was their inability to realise that a cannon can only shoot in a straight line, and that round towers and bastions and curved curtains could never be properly covered by defensive fire, however extravagant the number of gun-ports.

Deal Castle

Deal Castle is a fine and well preserved example of these formidable artillery forts, and the fact that it was not tested in war may be a tribute to its effectiveness as a deterrent, for the threat of invasion died away in a few splutterings off the Isle of Wight. Deal is a double clover-leaf in plan, with six lunettes or bastions in the outer and six in the inner curtain. It is interesting to notice that the fundamental principles of the concentric castle were revived here—the untenable courtyard which could be raked by fire from the inner bastions—which were separated from the 'keep' by an equally untenable passage-like court. The entire complex was sunk into the earth, and surrounded by a 56-feet-wide, flat-bottomed dry ditch whose outer revetted edge echoed exactly the shape of the outer curtain. There were five tiers of gun-ports or openings for small arms,

Deal Castle, as it might have appeared when newly completed in 1540

Sorrell 1959

145 in all. A contemporary complaint of artillery forts was that they 'stank of gunpowder and dogs' and leaving aside the canine nuisance, ventilation to carry away the fumes and smoke from the cannon must have been a major problem—the numerous ventilation shafts at Deal bear witness to this. The only approach to the castle is by way of a stone bridge over the ditch, and what was once a draw-bridge. The entrance passageway was complete with portcullis and five 'murder holes' in the roof, sufficient to have made Edwardian ghosts feel at home in an atmosphere not otherwise homely, for Deal had none of the splendours and graces of the medieval castles. The garrison was 24 men, and there could have been no lordly privacy—there *was* no lord, only a captain and a lieutenant—since all the rooms open into each other in a highly democratic fashion. The structure of the keep is remarkable, it is based on a central hollow pillar containing a well in the basement, and above that spiral stairs lead to the first floor and the roof. Although these artillery forts were built to cope with an emergency, the workmanship throughout is superb, and a wry and bitter humour has seen to it that much of the material used at Deal and in particular finely cut ashlar Caen stone notable for its pale colour, came from a recently-demolished monastery.

St Mawes Castle and Pendennis Castle

St Mawes Castle, one of the two forts (the other was Pendennis) covering the important Falmouth river and anchorage, was smaller than Deal, a single clover-leaf plan with three half-round bastions and a central round-tower. It was sited with extraordinary naïvety or incompetence (the terms are often synonymous in meaning) on the slope of a hill, so that it was utterly undefendable if attacked from the landward side, as it was in the Civil War, when it was taken by the Parliament forces without a shot being fired. St Mawes has been referred to as an 'architectural gem' than which there can be no cliché more suspect, but it is fair to say that St Mawes has a unity of design and perfection of workmanship which are impressive. A stone bridge and draw-bridge—now replaced by a fixed structure—span the rock-cut dry moat separating the castle from the hillside, and there was an octagonal guard house joined to an L-shaped building at the bridge end. On the edge of the rocks at the sea-side there still stands a half-round 'bulwark', a small fortification with three gun-ports, and this was later flanked by gun emplacements. On the westward side of the river stands Pendennis Castle on a steep sided flat-topped headland, and in every way it was a more serious work than St Mawes. The fundamental design is similar to Deal, but without the complicated system of lunettes: the round central 'keep' is 56 feet

(above) St Mawes Castle, now and as it might have appeared during the Civil War

Pendennis Castle, as it might have appeared when besieged in 1646

Pendennis Castle today

in diameter and 35 feet high, and the outer curtain is 30 feet away from the keep, circular in plan, but divided into 16 flat facets, each one with a gun-port. The observation turret is not placed centrally, but stands against what can only be described as the forebuilding, which connects the keep to the outer curtain and guards the bridge across the dry ditch. But the remarkable development at Pendennis is the large *enceinte* of fortified enclosure of between three and four acres, everywhere straight-sided, with projecting corner-bastions, and gun-ports so arranged that cannon could rake the long walls and reduce the escalade to a suicidal antic. This large scale Elizabethan reassessment of the requirements of fortification is of massive brick and masonry construction, and all the outer wall faces have a pronounced batter.

Southsea Castle

But 50 years before these later sixteenth century works, and almost before the cement was dry at Deal, Pendennis and St Mawes, a most important castle had been built at Southsea to guard the deep water channel into Portsmouth Harbour from mid-Solent. It was well advanced by June 1544, and a contemporary record attributes the design to 'his Majesty's own device'. The picture this presents of the King,

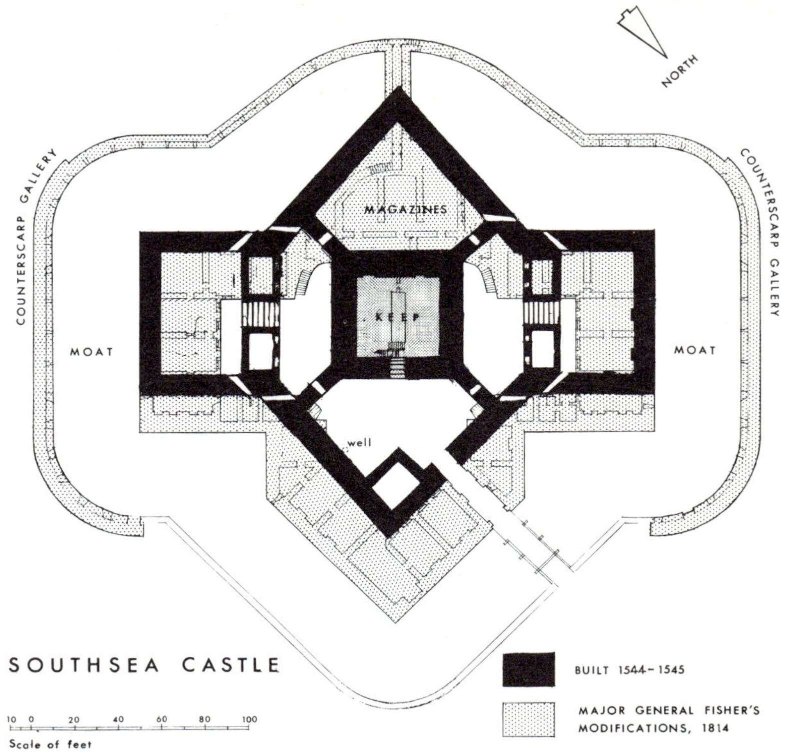

Southsea Castle, as it might have appeared in 1545

Alan Sorrell 1970

weighed down by his enormous corpulence, putting aside his domestic worries, manfully ignoring his complication of diseases and his ulcerated leg, neglecting even the persecution of Papists and Protestants, and quietly settling down to design a castle, is a pretty one. But whoever may have been responsible, Southsea Castle shows a quick and brilliant appreciation of the new problems of fortification: indeed, the instant turning away from the costly experiments at Deal and elsewhere show a royal ruthlessness typical of Henry, and not unlike his marital behaviour. Forts with angled bastions had been in existence in Italy and the eastern Mediterranean since the end of the fifteenth century, and what is surprising is not so much the abrupt change from the round to the square, but that the former type should ever have found favour. From this time there were to be no more round tower-keeps, and the interlocking circle and the clover-leaf design were abandoned almost as soon as they had come into being. At Southsea the principle of the angled bastion was adopted, with gun-ports so sited that all wall surfaces could be covered. The keep—the old name lives on—was square and squat and had a square corner turret, and almost the only resemblance to the other artillery forts was in the rounded contour of the parapets, designed to deflect cannon balls. There were rectangular gun-platforms to the east and west of the central keep: they were of solid earth construction and could be reached by steps from the courtyard; they were approximately half the height of the keep, and were independent defensive units complete with storehouses and magazines. Like Deal and the other Henrician forts (and unlike the medieval castle), Southsea had only one entrance, a simple round arch, and access was by way of a wooden bridge and a draw-bridge over the dry moat. So from Deal to Southsea and Pendennis the lesson of the cannonade had been learnt.

Everywhere, with the decline of the castle proper, the art of fortification had advanced with giant strides, propelled willy-nilly by the juggernaut cannon—and yet, despite the reason for it all, the result might be seen as a strange reversion to the geometrical simplicities of ancient times after the complicated pirouettes and fantasies of the Middle Ages.

The engineer responsible for the works of 1598 at Pendennis was a certain Gianibelli (who had already amplified and modernised the fort at Tilbury) and the great walled bailey with its keep and its inner courtyard brings us back almost to pre-Edwardian days. The wheel had revolved almost full circle, there was still a hard core, but the real strength lay once again in the hard outer-skin and the castle was now little more than a fortified camp. Whilst Henry was busily erecting his artillery forts and a little later Elizabeth was modernising in her economical way where she felt the need was greatest, diverse fates were overtaking the older castles in every part of the country. Some, in the northern counties and on the coasts were maintained as efficient defensive works, but the increasing security of life under a strong government persuaded many castle dwellers that wars and sieges were as old-fashioned as their castles, which they abandoned, and moved into new style mansions, where life was less restricted and more enjoyable. In many cases, of course, the old castles were given a new lease of life and embellished in the most splendid way so that the new was married to the old, this conjunction making, as at Raglan, an ideal setting for pageantry and display as well as comfort and convenience. But nowhere can there have been any real expectation of their future warlike use, and, therefore, the outbreak of the Civil War in 1642 must have been a shattering blow to a way of life that was rich in a cultural as well as a material way. For a short space of time these old castles flickered into their old life, but they all fell to cannonade or starvation. By the end of the war Britain had become a land of 'slighted' castles—the word has a contemptuous and derogatory sound—and humbled they were. A few survived, more or less intact, but ivy clad ruin was the usual fate, until recent times when conservation has preserved the mutilated fabric, but deprived it of the cherished romantic quality that was referred to at the beginning of this essay.

Tilbury Fort

Henry's forts did not play a very important part in the Civil War, probably because they had been designed to fight attack from the sea, and that did not materialise. The only famous siege was of Pendennis, which the Royalists bravely defended for five months, and only surrendered because of starvation. The garrison marched out with 'flying colours, trumpets sounding, drums beating' but so feeble were they that some of the men soon died after partaking of food. Their commander was Colonel John Arundell whose nickname was 'Old Tilbury' because he had been present there when Elizabeth made her famous speech in the year of the Armada. It is fitting that Tilbury should be mentioned, for there can be seen the final turn of the wheel and the return to the beginnings of fortification: it is no longer possible to use 'castle' as a descriptive term, it must be Tilbury Fort. The Fort defended the approach to London, where the river narrows suddenly to 800 yards, and it was the site of one of Henry's blockhouses, now totally disappeared but probably D-shape in plan and of no architectural significance. In 1588 Gianibelli hastily carried out defensive works, using Henry's blockhouse as the focal point, but the existing fortifications date from 1670 when Sir Bernard de Gomme, Charles II's Chief Engineer, completely remodelled

Tilbury Fort, as it might have appeared about 1725

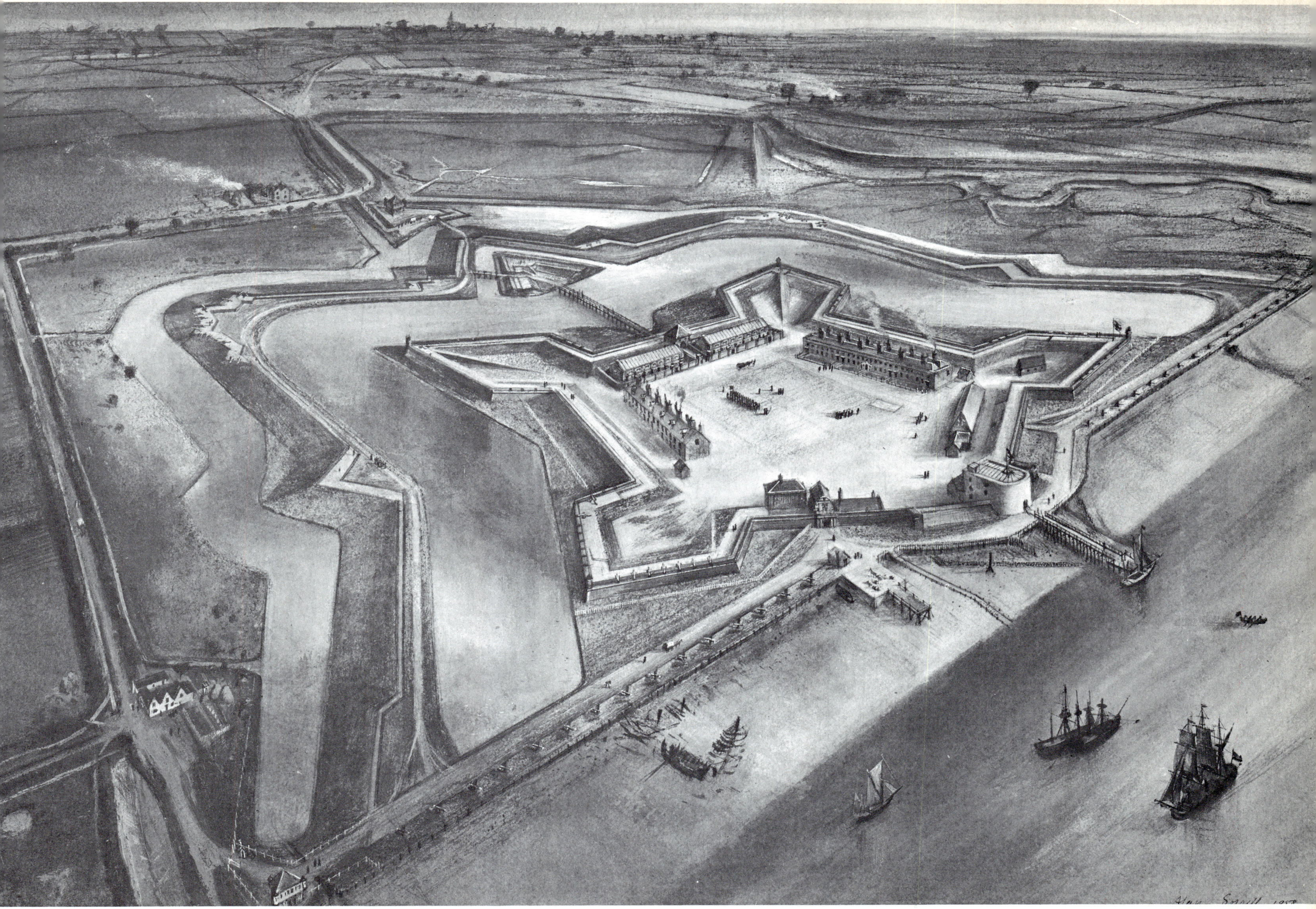

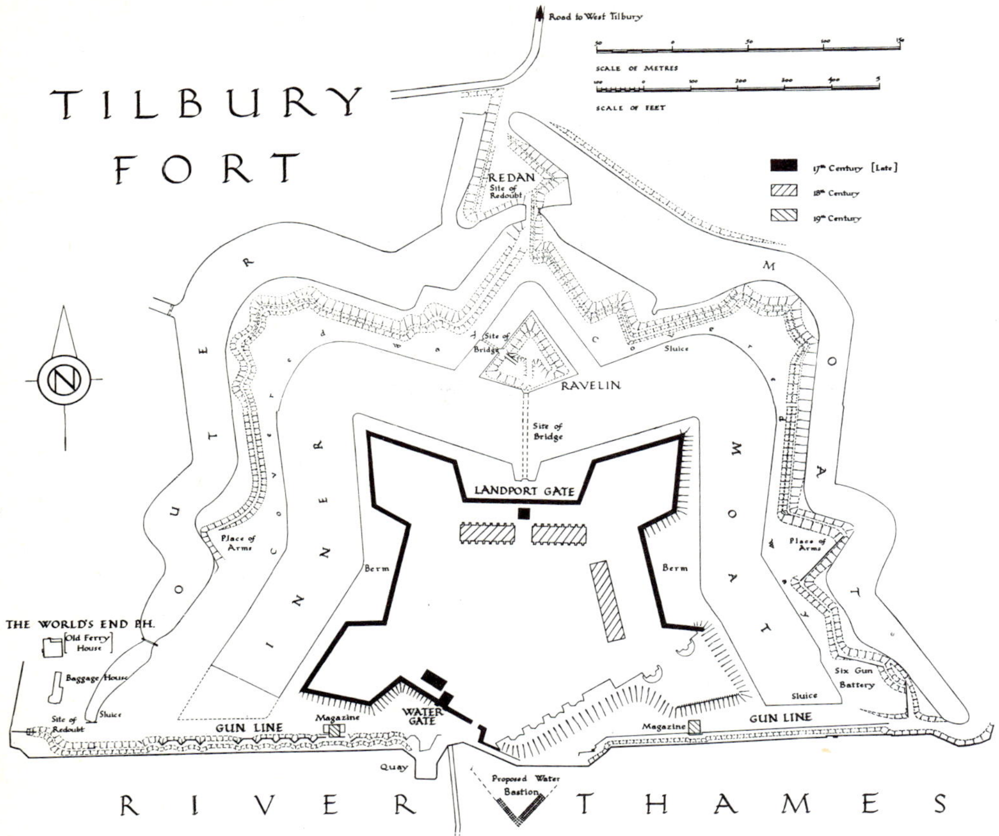

Fig. 3. Site plan of Fort and Outworks

the fort in accordance with up-to-date continental methods, with which the King had become familiar during his years of exile. The site is a flat one, with pale marshland, intersected by vein-like watercourses flowing into the Thames, and the low sprawling Essex hills to the north under the vast Essex sky. The fort, its base line on the riverbank, is roughly hexagonal in plan, and de Gomme retainéd the Henrician blockhouse as the focal point in his new system of bastioned fortification. There are two wide wet moats regulated by sluices, and all the outer works are sloping earth banks with angled bastions served by a 'covered way' so that troops could be rushed under cover to any threatened point. The inner defences are earth banks revetted in brick, and the corner bastions mounted cannon which covered the intervening walls and the flank of the adjacent bastion. A Redan—an outwork with two angled faces—protected the entrance over the outer moat, and was itself covered by spurs in the outer works, whose entire length was strengthened by a series of interlocking spurs and salients from which a damaging cross-fire could have been directed against the attacker. A ravelin—a fortified island—protected the inner moat and the wooden bridge which led to the Landport Gate. The parade ground was lined with barrack blocks, officers' quarters, powder magazines, guard house and chapel. Two formidable gun-lines east and west of Henry's blockhouse, with magazines and a redoubt completed the riverside fortifications, and with their heavy batteries formed the main defences of the river approach to London. Almost exactly 200 years after de Gomme's activities one last great programme of fortification took place in Britain, due to the emergence of powerful new weapons, and at Tilbury Captain Charles Gordon was the engineer in charge of the construction of new heavy batteries at the fort. There were to be no such cannon as these to defend Khartoum.

Through the centuries, from the fortified camps of ancient Egypt and Rome to the gradually evolving castle of medieval times, the profile changed greatly, from the low horizontal to the lofty towers with their gleaming pointed roofs, machicolations and battlements, and then, a rapid decline to the low bastions of Tilbury.

The Gothic vertical had reverted to the Classic horizontal. And the decline was not only in profile, but in function and feeling, for in ancient times there had been an altogether grim and no-nonsense feeling in camp and castle, but that gave place to a decorated extravagance in which there was a happy amalgam of strength and beauty. Then, at the crack of the cannon all this was changed and a progressive deterioration set in. New weapons and new conditions bred a new objectivity, or so it would seem: war was a stern business, there was no place for gallant knights and lovely ladies any more. So when the castle became once more the masculine fortified camp, any playful human quality disappeared. To be fair, de Gomme did allow himself one last gasp of frivolity at Tilbury in his charming Water Gate, and the King who is remembered more for his mistresses than for his military achievements must have liked it. But it is a very small voice singing a dying song.

If a legionary of old Rome could have returned from the shades and visited Tilbury Fort he would have felt quite at home there, and he would have been gratified to see that nothing had really changed in 1500 years.